LIBRARY OF CONGRESS

Music, Theater, Dance

AN ILLUSTRATED GUIDE

LIBRARY OF CONGRESS WASHINGTON 1993

This publication was made possible by generous support from the James Madison Council, a national, private-sector advisory council dedicated to helping the Library of Congress share its unique resources with the nation and the world.

Music, Theater, Dance is composed in Centaur, a typeface designed by American typographer and book designer Bruce Rogers (1870–1957). The full type font was first used at the Montague Press in 1915 for an edition of Maurice de Guérin's *The Centaur*.

Designers for this guide were Robert Wiser and Laurie Rosenthal, Meadows & Wiser, Washington, D.C.

COVER: *"L'enquerant plus n'eut joye ne bien,"* by an anonymous composer, in the *Chansonnier de M. le Marquis de Laborde*, fol. 56v–57r. This anthology of love songs was compiled in the late fifteenth century in France, probably in the Bourges-Orléans region. The fine miniatures and decoration are exceptionally lavish. *(Music Division)*

LIBRARY OF CONGRESS CATALOGING-IN-PUBLICATION DATA

Library of Congress.
      Library of Congress music, theater, dance : an illustrated guide.
         p. cm.
     ISBN 0-8444-0801-8
   ——— ——— Z663.37.L53 1993
     1. Library of Congress. Music Division. 2. Performing Arts Library (Washington, D.C.) 3. Music — Washington (D.C.) — Library resources. 4. Performing arts — Washington (D.C.) — Library resources. I. Title.
ML136.U5M92 1993
791'.09753 — dc20   93–27720
                                            CIP
                                            MN

For sale by the U.S. Government Printing Office
Superintendent of Documents
Mail Stop: SSOP, Washington, D.C. 20402–9328

Contents

THE MUSIC DIVISION—formally created in 1896 and established in quarters within the Library's Jefferson Building upon its completion in 1897—traces the origin of its collections to the thirteen books on music literature and theory that were contained in Thomas Jefferson's library, purchased by the Congress in 1815. At that time, the cultivation and development of a music library were scarcely matters of great importance. By the closing years of the century, however, some 400,000 music items had been added to the Library's collections, largely effected through the deposits under the Copyright Act. Today, the Music Division's collections number close to eight million items, including the classified music and book collections, music and literary manuscripts, microforms, and copyright deposits.

In his annual report for 1897, Librarian of Congress John Russell Young wrote that "This [music] department is as yet an experiment, but there is reason to believe that with proper care ... it may become one of the most important...." A year later, in his report for 1898, Mr. Young said that the new department of music's "... growth thus far has resulted in the foundation of what is destined to be one of the great musical libraries of the world ...," and that "Music in its best sense is a science belonging to all ages, as well as all nationalities and conditions of men, and the Library of Congress should contain its earliest as well as its latest and most complete expression." These prescient remarks have been, and continue to be, fulfilled, and indeed have provided touchstones for the Library's cultivation of the art and study of music in all its aspects.

As the vision of Librarian John Russell Young was remarkable, so was that of Oscar George Theodore Sonneck, appointed chief of the now recognized Music Division in 1902. Through his extraordinary energy and wisdom, he charted a course for organizing the collections and for vigorous acquisitions programs that has been sustained for nine decades.

Beyond showing the highlights of the collections of music that have been assembled over the years, this guide also reveals the single most important change in the Music Division's mission that has evolved since the opening of the present century: the addition of musical performance and the creation of new music. Elizabeth Sprague Coolidge and Gertrude Clarke Whittall, within the span of a decade, 1925–1935, established through their philanthropy to the American people unrivaled means for concerts and commissions that continue to flourish, and indeed have spawned similar foundations in the Library for the art of music. The Library of Congress is unique among national libraries in that it embraces the complete range of music—from creating new works to having them

Geraldine Farrar. Portrait by Friedrich August von Kaulbach. Oil on canvas. In later life, Farrar wrote of this painting: "I hated to sit for my picture; even a quick photo was a chore. As I recall with von Kaulbach, we enlivened the sitting hours with matters of the moment, musical and artistic. . . . These sittings lasted from an hour to three or four, according to the light and discretion of the artist. I was then of such lively temperament that an induced position after a time would get artificial to my mind, and I would beg for a little diversion and walk about the studio." (*Geraldine Farrar Collection*)

performed and placing the original manuscripts in the collections in perpetuity, for the use of succeeding generations. The circle is complete in many cases when the new work is chosen for recording, and thus for even wider dissemination to artists, scholars, and music lovers.

Mrs. Coolidge and Mrs. Whittall, beyond their foundations created for musical performance, commissioning, and scholarship, gave magnificent collections of manuscripts that they had collected in the course of their devotion to music. With their gifts of musical materials—including Mrs. Whittall's Stradivari instruments—they instantly placed magnets in the collections that have drawn hundreds of other rich collections to the Music Division, additions that range from Aaron Copland's *Rodeo* to the Guarneri violin of Fritz Kreisler, from Leonard Bernstein's *West Side Story* to George Gershwin's *An American in Paris,* from Benjamin Britten's *Peter Grimes* to William Schuman's *The Mighty Casey,* and from Jerome Kern's *Show Boat* to Rodgers and Hammerstein's *Oklahoma!* The generous spirits of Mrs. Coolidge and Mrs. Whittall continue to find expression in succeeding generations of benefactors.

Not only is music research and study carried forward in the Music Division, but also research in theater and dance. Staff specialists in theater and dance guide readers to materials housed in the Music Division as well as elsewhere in the Library's collections. The sections on theater and dance in this guide reflect the Library's growing commitment to a broad interpretation of the performing arts.

Contributors of chapters to this guide comprise Gail L. Freunsch, Oxana Horodecka, Anne E. McLean, Robert E. Sheldon, Wayne D. Shirley, Raymond A. White, Vicky Wulff, and Walter Zvonchenko.

Benjamin Britten. *(Aaron Copland Collection) (Photograph by Andrée Vilas)*

OPPOSITE. Serge Koussevitzky. *(Serge Koussevitzky Collection) (Photograph by Arthur Griffin)*

JAMES W. PRUETT, CHIEF
MUSIC DIVISION

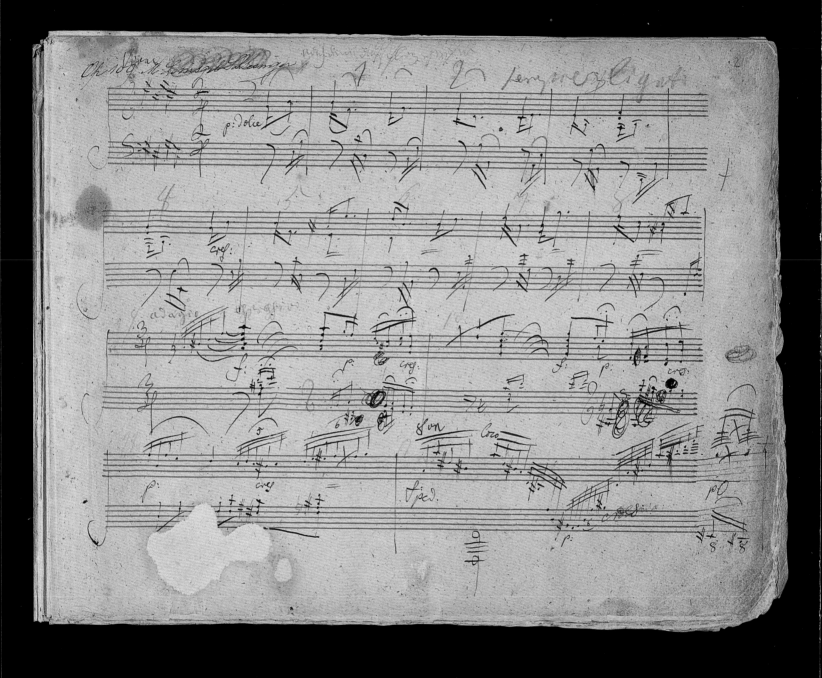

Special Collections of the Music Division

THE SPECIAL COLLECTIONS OF THE MUSIC DIVISION constitute a resource for musical scholarship which is unmatched anywhere in the world. These unique bodies of materials are extraordinarily vast and diverse, yet very much interrelated. They include some of the greatest treasures of the Music Division and, indeed, of the Library of Congress.

Perhaps the most immediately striking feature of these Special Collections is the sheer quantity of items which they contain. The Music Division currently holds more than five hundred named collections which vary in size from fewer than a dozen items to more than a half-million. The Serge Koussevitzky Collection includes manuscript and printed music scores, correspondence, financial records, iconography, and concert programs totaling more than 300,000 items. The Irving Berlin Collection, Berlin's personal papers as well as business records, contains approximately 750,000 items. The archives of Boston music publisher A. P. Schmidt contain nearly one hundred boxes of correspondence and more than three hundred boxes of music scores.

Impressive, too, is the diversity of materials in these collections. They contain quite literally millions of items in an enormous variety of formats: music manuscripts, printed music, correspondence and other literary manuscripts, books, pamphlets, concert programs, posters, playbills, newspaper and magazine clippings, business records, scrapbooks, photographs, drawings, etchings, paintings, bronze and plaster busts, certificates, citations, medals and honors, audio and video recordings, and artifacts which range from the Library's famed Stradivari stringed instruments to a lock of Beethoven's hair, and from George Gershwin's first metronome to Victor Herbert's death mask.

Within the collections one frequently finds music materials that document various stages of the compositional process. Many works are represented by autograph manuscripts—sketches, early drafts, complete scores; for some works there are manuscripts in the hand of copyists and arrangers; in some cases, first edition scores and proof copies are present.

Most of the items in the special collections are unique; others are extremely rare. Present are photographs of which no other copies are known; as well, there are printed scores and textual materials of which very few copies are extant.

The holdings of the Music Division span more than eight hundred years of Western music history and practice. The vast majority of the items in the Special Collections date, however, from the past two and one-half centuries. Particular areas of strength are American music, chamber music, opera, and American musical theater.

OPPOSITE. Ludwig van Beethoven. *Sonata für Hammerklavier ...* [Sonata in E-major, Op. 109]. Autograph keyboard score. *(Gertrude Clarke Whittall Foundation Collection)*

SUCCESSIVE PAGES. PAGE 10. Benjamin Britten and Montagu Slater. *Peter Grimes,* Op. 33. Section from *Interlude IV: Passacaglia.* Autograph full orchestral-vocal score. *(Serge Koussevitzky Music Foundation Collection) (London, New York Boosey & Hawkes, 1945)*

PAGE 11 LEFT. George Gershwin, Ira Gershwin, and DuBose Heyward. Introduction to *Porgy and Bess,* First page of the autograph full orchestral-vocal score. *(George and Ira Gershwin Collection) (From* Porgy and Bess *by George Gershwin, DuBose and Dorothy Heyward, and Ira Gershwin. Used by permission of George Gershwin Music, DuBose and Dorothy Heyward Memorial Fund Publishing, and Ira Gershwin Music)*

PAGE 11 RIGHT. George (top) and Ira Gershwin. Self-portraits. *(George and Ira Gershwin Collection)*

INTRODUCTION- PORGY AND BESS.

George Gershwin.

ALLEGRO CON BRIO   RISOLUTO e BEN MARCATO

Orchestration begun late 1934 —
finished Sept. 2, 1935.

ABOVE. Jascha Heifetz. *(Jascha Heifetz Collection)* *(Photograph by John Bryson)* *(This photograph appears with the kind permission of the Heifetz family.)*

OPPOSITE UPPER LEFT. Sergei Rachmaninoff. *(Rachmaninoff Archives)* *(Photograph by Eric Schaal)*

OPPOSITE UPPER RIGHT. Irving Berlin. *(Irving Berlin Collection)*

OPPOSITE LOWER LEFT. Artur Rubinstein. *(Photograph by RCA Records)*

OPPOSITE LOWER RIGHT. Irving Berlin. Typescript draft for the lyric *Anything You Can Do* from *Annie Get Your Gun. (Irving Berlin Collection)*

Many of the collections consist of personal papers of such figures as composers Sergei Rachmaninoff and Victor Herbert, violinists Fritz Kreisler and Jascha Heifetz, singers Helen Traubel and Geraldine Farrar, pianists Artur Rubinstein and Leopold Godowsky, choreographer Franziska Boas, and musicologist Nicolas Slonimsky. Other collections document the work of two or more individuals such as composer and lyricist George and Ira Gershwin, composer/musicologist and composer/educator Charles and Ruth Crawford Seeger, choreographer/director and dancer/singer Bob Fosse and Gwen Verdon, the members of the Budapest String Quartet, and the Damrosch family of musicians. Although most of these archives comprise materials in a variety of formats including music manuscripts, correspondence, photographs, and the like, some collections, such as those of composers Samuel Barber and William Schuman, contain only music manuscripts and libretto materials.

Other collections represent the work of a scholar or collector. The Dayton C. Miller Flute Collection contains not only more than 1,600 flutes, making it one of the world's largest collections devoted to a single musical instrument, but also music scores, books, and a multitude of other materials relating to the flute. The Albert Schatz Collection, purchased by the Library in 1909, contains more than 12,000 opera libretti, principally from the seventeenth, eighteenth, and nineteenth centuries. This significant acquisition helped set the stage for developing the collections in ensuing decades; it is a continuing touchstone for the Library's efforts to acquire important materials for study and research in music. The Moldenhauer Archives at the Library of Congress contain an extraordinary collection of autograph music manuscripts and correspondence dating from medieval times to the present; particularly strong are its holdings of Brahms and Webern, but its greatest interest lies in individual gems such as the autograph scores of Bloch's *Schelomo*, the coronation scene from *Boris Godunov* in Rimsky-Korsakov's arrangement, or the sketches for the slow movement of Beethoven's *Piano Sonata, Op. 28/2*. The Charles Jahant Collection consists of more than 2,000 photographs of opera singers from the nineteenth and twentieth centuries. The Heineman Foundation Collection in Honor of Edward N. Waters and the Rosenthal Collection are particularly rich in the autograph music and letters of Franz Liszt. Mr. Waters, a member of the staff of the Music Division for more than thirty-five years and its chief from 1972 until 1976, had a lifelong interest in the Hungarian composer, and his scholarship was gen-

```
deeper
lower
faster
writer
brighter
darker
smaller
bigger
tougher

        I can drink a schooner
        I can do it# sooner
        You'd get sick on liquor
        You'd get even sicker          (I can do most anything)
        ##################################  #############
        ############################      Canyou bake a pie
        ####                              No
        #################################  Neither can I

I can wear a girdle
Not without a hurdle
l can be a mother
Not without the other
Can you open up a safe            Could
Yes                          I ### live on bread and cheese
Without being caught             And only on that?
Yes                              Yes
That's what I thought.           So can a rat

        Could
     I #### die a########## mythrs death
        and hang from a rope
        Yes
        That's what I hope              i'd be good at spying
                                        That I'm not deneighing
     I reduce my upper
     After every supper
     I get even thinner
     After every dinner
     I could live on bread and cheese
     And only on that
     Yes
     So can a rat.
     Anything you can say I can say softer
     I can say anything softer than you.
```

"ANNIE GET YOUR GUN"

erously supplemented by the philanthropy of Dannie N. and James H. Heineman and Harry Rosenthal.

Fewer in number but of great importance are the collections that derive from musical organizations and foundations. Particularly significant is the archive of the Elizabeth Sprague Coolidge Foundation, which, since the 1920s, has produced an unequalled legacy of commissions and performances. The Coolidge Collection contains not only the autograph manuscripts for many of the most important chamber works of this century, including Aaron Copland's *Appalachian Spring*, George Crumb's *Ancient Voices of Children*, Paul Hindemith's *Hérodiade*, Sergei Prokofiev's *String Quartet, Op. 50*, and Igor Stravinsky's *Apollon-Musagète*, but also correspondence and other materials relating to their composition and performance. Also among the numerous extraordinary manuscripts in this collection are Samuel Barber's *Hermit Songs*, Bartók's *Fifth String Quartet*, Ravel's *Chansons madécasses*, Webern's *String Quartet, Op. 28*, and Schoenberg's *Third* and *Fourth String Quartet*. As well, Mrs. Coolidge's own life as musical philanthropist and impresario is richly documented, especially through her extensive correspondence with friends and colleagues, performers and composers.

Similarly, the archives of the Serge Koussevitzky Music Foundation contain scores and related materials which document an extraordinary commissioning program, begun in the 1940s and responsible for such masterworks as Bartók's *Concerto for Orchestra* and Benjamin Britten's *Peter Grimes*; and among the American composers: Copland, *Third Symphony*; and David Diamond, *Fourth Symphony*; Roger Sessions, *Third Symphony*; and William Schuman, *Symphony for Strings*. In addition, the collection contains the personal papers of Koussevitzky, conductor of the Boston Symphony Orchestra and founder of the Berkshire Music Center at Tanglewood, Massachusetts. More recently established, the McKim Fund, underwriting the composition and performance of works for violin and piano, has generated a strong collection of late-twentieth-century manuscripts in the McKim Fund Collection, including works by William Bolcom, Elliott Carter, and Gunther Schuller.

The Gertrude Clarke Whittall Collection contains the five Stradivari instruments that Mrs. Whittall gave to the Library in 1935–1936 as well as materials which relate to the concert activities of the Whittall Foundation. In addition, the collection contains an extraordinary group of autograph music manuscripts and letters of such preeminent composers as Bach, Mozart, Haydn, Beethoven, Schubert, Mendelssohn, Brahms, and Schoenberg, purchased for the Library by Mrs. Whittall.

OPPOSITE. Leonard Bernstein. *(Aaron Copland Collection) (Photographic proof sheet by Victor Kraft)*

ABOVE LEFT. Igor Stravinsky. *Agon*. Composer's autograph reduction for two pianos. Commissioned by Lincoln Kirstein and George Balanchine, *Agon* was composed and revised by Stravinsky at various times in the period 1953–1957. The first stage performance by the New York City Ballet was on December 1, 1957, with choreography by Balanchine. *(London, New York, Boosey & Hawkes, 1957)*

ABOVE RIGHT. Igor Stravinsky. *(Fritz Steinbach Collection)*

OPPOSITE. Aaron Copland. *(Aaron Copland Collection)*

Not surprising, but impressive nonetheless, are the remarkable ways in which the Special Collections in Music are interrelated: the web of personal and professional relationships in the world of music is intricate, widespread, and finely cast, and the Library's collections clearly represent that world. For example, although the greater part of the Aaron Copland materials is found in the Copland Collection, manuscripts of works commissioned by the Coolidge and Koussevitzky Foundations are in those collections, and the manuscript of a work written for Vernon Duke is in the Duke Collection. Likewise, while most of the George and Ira Gershwin materials are in the Gershwin Collection, two manuscripts of the *Rhapsody in Blue* are in the Ferde Grofé Collection (Grofé made the original orchestrations of that work), and lyric sheets for five songs written by Ira Gershwin and Vernon Duke are found in the Duke Collection.

Comparable is the interrelation of correspondence of musical figures. Letters of Carl Engel, musicologist and chief of the Music Division from 1922 until 1934, are found in twenty-six special collections; letters of composer Henry Cowell are found in twenty-three; and letters of Marian Nevins MacDowell, wife of composer Edward MacDowell and founder of the MacDowell Colony, are found in seventeen.

Perhaps more intricate are the links that may be found between the collections assembled by scholars and collectors. For example, the Music Division holds the world's largest aggregation of autograph manuscripts of Johannes Brahms, although there is no single special collection known as the "Brahms Collection." The largest numbers of Brahms manuscripts are to be found in the Whittall Collection and the Moldenhauer Archives, with additional manuscripts in the Damrosch-Blaine, Selden-Goth, and Heineman Foundation Collections. Similarly, autograph manuscripts of Franz Liszt are housed in the Rosenthal, Seldon-Goth, Batchelder, Adler, Menter, Morgan, and Heineman Foundation Collections and in the Moldenhauer Archives.

If the art of music can be described as continuous and evolutionary, so, too, can we consider the Special Collections in the Music Division. Even as this guide is being written, musicians across the country and around the world continue to compose, perform, and study music, and the Music Division pursues its initiatives to acquire, organize, and preserve new materials. Thus, these Special Collections, which are at once subjects of and resources for musical scholarship, become not only monuments to the music of the past but integral parts of the music of the future.

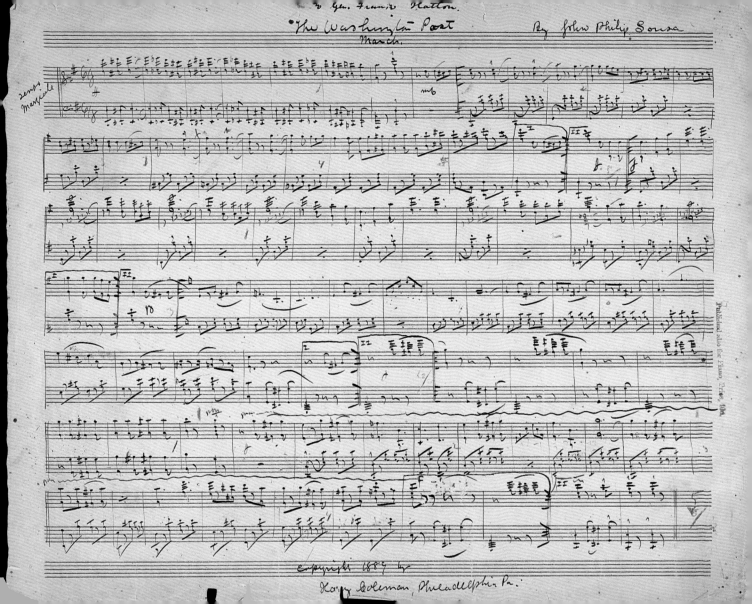

The Washington Post
March

By John Philip Sousa

Published also for Piano. Price, 40¢

Foundations
for Music

Two extraordinary American women, Elizabeth Sprague Coolidge and Gertrude Clarke Whittall, by their generosity toward the Library of Congress Music Division, had a profound influence on the history of music in the United States and laid the cornerstone for all subsequent musical philanthropy in the Library. They were born within three years of one another, and their support of music in the Library overlapped for several decades, beginning in the 1930s. Although their devotion to music was equal, they expressed that devotion in divergent but complementary ways, Mrs. Coolidge focusing largely on the new, Mrs. Whittall on the classic tradition exemplified by the repertory of the string quartet.

Elizabeth Sprague Coolidge (1864–1953), one of the most notable patrons in the history of American music, seized an opportunity in 1924 to expand the vision and mission of the Library of Congress through underwriting concerts, commissioning new music, and encouraging musicological scholarship. Having already won international prominence by sponsoring chamber music festivals in Pittsfield, Massachusetts, and for commissioning and inspiring compositions by eminent contemporary composers in the United States and abroad, she sought to establish a permanent base for these activities as well as a permanent musical influence.

In 1925 the Elizabeth Sprague Coolidge Foundation was established in the Library for the promotion and advancement of chamber music through commissions, public concerts, and festivals. Mrs. Coolidge's ultimate aim, as stated in a letter dated February 4, 1925, to the Librarian of Congress, Herbert Putnam, was profound as well as prescient:

to make possible, through the Library of Congress, the composition and performance of music in ways which might otherwise be considered too unique or too expensive to be ordinarily undertaken. Not this alone, of course, nor with a view to extravagance for its own sake; but as an occasional possibility of giving precedence to considerations of quality over those of quantity; to artistic rather than to economic values; and to opportunity over expediency.

The Library of Congress Trust Fund Board, the first of its kind in the federal government, was established in 1925 to administer the funds of the Elizabeth Sprague Coolidge Foundation and all future endowments. With an additional gift, also in 1925, Mrs. Coolidge financed the construction of the 511-seat Coolidge Auditorium in the northwest courtyard of the Jefferson Building. Designed according to her preference for "severe and chaste beauty" rather than "ornate display," the Coolidge Auditorium was completed just in time for the first Coolidge

Elizabeth Sprague Coolidge. *(Elizabeth Sprague Coolidge Collection)*

20

Elizabeth Sprague Coolidge.

Festival, which successfully inaugurated the new hall on October 28, 1925. This structure has become world famous for its magnificent acoustical properties, for the caliber of the artists and ensembles who have played there, for newly commissioned works premiered, and for the individually scheduled concerts interspersed among concert series, retrospectives, and festivals.

Elizabeth Sprague Coolidge's legacy lies not only in the Foundation, auditorium, and concerts, but also in the collections she presented to the Library of original manuscripts and papers that she had received through her philanthropic activities. As a result of the Coolidge commissions executed by eminent composers, a steady stream of notable holographs has reached the Library through the years; many composers maintained a special relationship with the Library and continued to make generous donations of their own manuscripts.

Following the standards set by Mrs. Coolidge's generosity, Gertrude Clarke Whittall (1867–1965), another great philanthropist, presented to the Library in 1935–1936 five incomparable Stradivari instruments, as well as a Tourte bow for each instrument. (See the chapter "The Collections of Musical Instruments" for details on these instruments.) In February 1936, the Gertrude Clarke Whittall Foundation was established at the Library to maintain the Stradivari instruments and to support their use in concerts. For several years, guest string quartets played on the instruments for one or more concerts until the Library settled on the idea of a resident ensemble: the Budapest String Quartet was the Library's resident quartet from 1940–1962, and from 1962 to the present, the Juilliard String Quartet.

Continuing her generosity to the Library, in

Johann Sebastian Bach. *Festo visitationis Mariae: Meine Seel erhebt den Herren* (1724) (Feast of the Visitation of Mary: My Soul doth magnify the Lord) (BWV 10/BC A175). Autograph full orchestral-vocal score. *Meine Seel* is the fifth in Bach's second cycle of cantatas for the church year which began on the First Sunday after Trinity, June 11, 1724. This manuscript is a "composing score," that is, it contains numerous corrections, rejected passages, and, on occasion, marginal sketches of a tentative nature. The text is taken directly, and in paraphrase, from Luke I, 46–55. *(Gertrude Clarke Whittall Foundation Collection)*

OPPOSITE. Gertrude Clarke Whittall. Painted miniature by Laura Hills. *(Gertrude Clarke Whittall Foundation Collection)*

1938 Mrs. Whittall provided funds for the construction of the Whittall Pavilion, a drawing room intended as a "beautiful sanctuary of the precious Stradivari," adjoining the foyer of the Coolidge Auditorium. To complete her gift and to enhance the value of the Stradivari, Mrs. Whittall also presented to the Library a remarkable assemblage of original manuscripts by composers such as Haydn, Mozart, Beethoven, Brahms, and Schoenberg.

Since 1925, when the Coolidge Foundation was established, additional foundations have been created through gift or bequest, permitting the Library to extend significantly its influence in the musical world. Throughout the years, the generosity of donors has enabled the Library to render exceptional service to the public and the world of music through performances, commissions, acquisitions, broadcasts, recordings, exhibits, lectures, and publications, as well as other related activities.

Among the Library's music foundations that perpetuate the art and scholarship of music are:

The SERGE KOUSSEVITZKY MUSIC FOUNDATION IN THE LIBRARY OF CONGRESS, inaugurated in 1949, is allied with the Koussevitzky Music Foundation, Inc., established earlier — in 1942 — by the eminent Russian conductor, Serge Koussevitzky. Dedicated to the development of creative musical talent, the Foundation has commissioned over 250 composers and seeks to encourage the dissemination of their scores by performance and other means. Original manuscripts of the works commissioned by the two Foundations are placed in the Serge Koussevitzky Foundation Collection in the Library.

Established in 1968 by Katie Louchheim, onetime Deputy Assistant Secretary of State for Public Affairs, and her husband, an investment banker and presidential advisor, the KATIE AND WALTER LOUCHHEIM FUND provides support especially for broadcasting the Library's chamber music concerts.

The MCKIM FUND (Leonora Jackson and W. Duncan McKim) was created in 1970 through a bequest of Mrs. W. Duncan McKim, a concert violinist, who won international prominence under her maiden name, Leonora Jackson. W. Duncan McKim was a distinguished authority in the fields of medicine and philosophy as well as an organist. Income from this endowment is used for the creation and appreciation of music for violin and piano.

The DA CAPO FUND, begun by an anonymous donor in 1978, supports concerts, lectures, publications, seminars, and other activities which parallel and enrich scholarly research in music using items from the collections of the Music Division of unique artistic or human appeal.

Leonora Jackson McKim. (*Leonora Jackson McKim Collection*)

Sergei Prokofiev. String Quartet, Op. 50. Full autograph score. Prokofiev wrote in his "short" autobiography of 1941: "Before starting work on the quartet [in 1930], I studied Beethoven's quartets, chiefly in railway carriages on my way from one concert to another. In this way, I came to understand and greatly admire his quartet technique. Perhaps this explains the somewhat 'classical' idiom of the first movement of my quartet ... The first performance of the quartet took place in Washington on 23 April 1931. Besides this, the Roth Quartet was sent to Europe with a programme of music written for the Library of Congress, and, on 9 October 1931, played my quartet for the first time in Moscow." *(Elizabeth Sprague Coolidge Foundation Collection)*

The MAE AND IRVING JUROW FUND was founded in 1980 by Mae Jurow, professional artist, and Irving Jurow, eminent lawyer, vice-president and general counsel of a pharmaceutical company, to support chamber music concerts in which the harpsichord is the featured instrument. New music for harpsichord is also a part of the Fund's purposes.

The BORIS AND SONYA KROYT MEMORIAL FUND was established in 1980 by Yanna Kroyt Brandt and Nathan Brandt in memory of her mother, Sonya, and father, Boris Kroyt, the illustrious violist of the famous Budapest String Quartet, to present concerts each year featuring the talents of gifted but not yet widely known musicians and to support concert broadcasts and recordings.

The WILLIAM AND ADELINE CROFT MEMORIAL FUND began in 1990 to enhance the chamber music series, to enlarge the audience for chamber music through broadcasting, to enrich the Library's collections of musical rarities, and to produce and distribute recordings. Like so many of the Library's benefactors, William Croft, a renowned lawyer, and Adeline Ritschel Croft, a noted pianist and teacher, were devoted followers of the Library's concerts and regular, enthusiastic members of the audience.

The ROSE MARIE AND HAROLD SPIVACKE FUND was created in 1982 by Rose Marie Spivacke, in memory of her husband Harold Spivacke—musicologist, music librarian, and a distinguished former chief of the Music Division from 1937–1972—to acquire books, manuscripts, and other materials for the collections of the Library.

The KINDLER FOUNDATION TRUST FUND was established in 1983 by the Kindler Foundation (incorporated in 1952) to offer concerts and to commission new chamber music in memory of Hans Kindler (1892–1949), Dutch-American cellist, conductor, and founder of the National Symphony Orchestra of Washington, D.C.

The ISENBERGH CLARINET FUND was initiated in 1985 by Max Isenbergh, prominent attorney, law professor, and accomplished amateur clarinet player in memory of his sister, Charlotte Isenbergh Kessler, primarily to support public concerts featuring the clarinet.

The MOLDENHAUER ARCHIVES FOUNDATION AT THE LIBRARY OF CONGRESS was established in 1988 by the bequest of Hans Moldenhauer (1906–1987), pianist, teacher, author, and founder of the Moldenhauer Archives for the study of music history from primary sources located in the Library of Congress and nine sister institutions throughout the world. The funds from this Foundation are used to augment the Moldenhauer Archives at the Library, to

Quartet

I

Serge Prokofieff, op. 50.
1930

Allegro

publish books and facsimiles based on the Archives, and to commission new musical compositions based on materials in these Archives.

The Moldenhauer bequest, further supplemented with major manuscripts acquired in 1988 from Mary Moldenhauer, his widow, is the greatest composite gift of music materials ever to be received by the Library. It consists of autograph music manuscripts, letters, and documents spanning the history of musical creativity from the twelfth century to modern times.

The ROSE AND MONROE VINCENT FUND was established in 1990 by Monroe Vincent, noted scientist, author, and amateur violist. The fund assists in offering concerts at the Library, supports the Library's endeavors to bring these concerts to a wider audience through broadcasting, recordings, related publications, and other communications media as may be developed in the future.

Through her testamentary bequest, the GERSHWIN FUND was established by Leonore S. Gershwin in 1992 to perpetuate the name and works of Ira Gershwin (1896–1983), librettist and lyricist, and George Gershwin (1898–1937), American composer, pianist, and conductor, and to provide support for worthy related music and literary projects. Mrs. Gershwin, widow of Ira Gershwin, was among the strongest supporters of the Library for many years. She purchased important manuscripts, papers, and letters for the Gershwin Collection, sponsored gala concerts of music by the Gershwins, and established a collaboration with the Library through the Leonore Gershwin/Library of Congress Recording and Publication Project, which is producing authoritative recordings and editions of the Gershwins' music.

The ANNE ADLUM HULL AND WILLIAM REMSEN STRICKLAND FUND was created in 1992 by William Remsen Strickland, noted American conductor and recipient of numerous awards, for the promotion and advancement of American music, through lectures, publications, commissions, concerts of chamber music and radio broadcasts, and recordings.

The CAROLYN ROYALL JUST FUND dates from 1992, and was initiated through a bequest of Carolyn Royall Just, a distinguished attorney in Washington, D.C., who also performed with the George Washington University Symphony and with the Shoestring Orchestra, for performing or broadcasting concerts of classical chamber music.

The Library's widely acknowledged leadership in creating, performing, and collecting music for the benefit of the nation has been linked for decades to the generosity and wisdom of benefactors. These philanthropists continue to sustain the artistic values that music holds, and help assure the future of all musical art.

Béla Bartók. *Concerto for Orchestra.* List of timings, and first page of the autograph full orchestral score. Completed in 1943, and later revised in 1945, the *Concerto* was commissioned by the Koussevitzky Music Foundation. It was premiered by the Boston Symphony Orchestra under the baton of Koussevitzky on December 1, 1944. The *Concerto* is one of the early commissions by the Foundation; part of a series of distinguished works from twentieth-century composers. *(Serge Koussevitzky Music Foundation Collection) (London, New York, Boosey & Hawkes, 1946)*

Public Events and Publications

For almost seven decades, the Music Division of the Library of Congress has presented an extraordinary series of chamber music concerts that have literally made music history, setting international standards for performance, composition, and broadcasting. Our concerts have featured artists whose names are now legendary—Gregor Piatigorsky, Artur Rubinstein, the Budapest String Quartet, George Szell, Nadia Boulanger, Clifford Curzon, Nathan Milstein, Leopold Stokowski, Claudio Arrau, Leonard Bernstein, Leontyne Price, the Juilliard String Quartet, the Beaux Arts Trio, and many others. Our broadcast series is the nation's oldest, and the first of its kind to be heard nationwide; commissions from Music Division foundations have become standards of the international concert repertoire. Lectures, symposia, and festivals sponsored by the Music Division have attracted participants from around the world and enlarged the art and scholarship of music. In recent years, the scope of these public programs has expanded to include exhibits, facsimile publications, and recordings.

While the last quarter century has seen an astounding blossoming of chamber music of all kinds in the United States, it is the Library of Congress that claims just title as the first national venue for creating, presenting, and preserving chamber music—an unbroken and continuing tradition of excellence. That tradition has encouraged present-day benefactors to join earlier philanthropists in supporting further commissions, concerts, and collections of musical manuscripts and documentary archives.

Elizabeth Sprague Coolidge founded the Library's concert series in 1925 with the gift of funds to build the Coolidge Auditorium, the site of more than 2,000 concerts to date. Her vision, dedication, and generosity opened the way for the Library to establish a tradition of excellence in the performance of chamber music in America. Mrs. Coolidge was noted for her patronage of chamber music competitions, performances, and festivals throughout the United States and Europe; since 1925, Coolidge Foundation presentations have helped to place the Library of Congress at the forefront of American cultural institutions.

In 1935, Gertrude Clarke Whittall gave the Library a quartet of Stradivari instruments; later, with the addition of a fifth instrument, she endowed a foundation to ensure their use in public concerts; through radio broadcasts, these instruments would soon be heard by a large national audience, played first by the Budapest String Quartet, and later by the Juilliard String Quartet, which inherited the Budapest's legacy as artists-in-residence. In 1982 the Beaux Arts Trio became the second ensemble to take up residence at the Library.

Throughout its history the Music Division's chamber series has balanced

The Juilliard String Quartet, Quartet in Residence at the Library of Congress, with the Library's Stradivarius stringed instruments on the stage of the Coolidge Auditorium. *(Photograph by Chad Evans Wyatt)*

Sound recordings issued by the Music Division. *(Photograph by Jim Higgins)*

strong commitments to both the traditional repertoire and to music by American composers, with an emphasis on new compositions. Aaron Copland, Samuel Barber, and Ned Rorem are but three of the many composers who have appeared at the Library as performers in premieres of their own works. The McKim Fund, established by the violinist Leonora Jackson McKim, has commissioned forty-five works for violin and piano from American composers. Since 1984, concerts celebrating the Division's Special Collections have showcased music by George and Ira Gershwin, Jerome Kern, Richard Rodgers, and other important figures of the American musical theater. The 1992–1993 season inaugurated a new jazz series, with a concert devoted to the music of Charles Mingus.

BROADCASTING

The Music Division's is the oldest chamber music broadcast series in the United States, with a long and distinguished history going back more than sixty years to the early days of broadcasting in this country. Trial broadcasts began as early as 1930, from the NBC studios in New York; the first live, national broadcast from the Coolidge Auditorium came three years later, on April 24, 1933: the first American appearance of the Adolf Busch String Quartet, performing works by Beethoven, Busch, and Pizzetti. By the early 1940s the Music Division had established the first international broadcasts of chamber music, with Canada and Latin America as the first recipients. Regular weekly broadcasts began with the 1948 season, and have continued without interruption to the present.

Concerts from the Library of Congress now reaches millions of listeners around the world, distributed via satellite to 120 U.S. cities each season through the American Public Radio Network. Since 1990, a special series of archival broadcasts has featured some of the historic moments from Library concerts—Leontyne Price performing with Samuel Barber, the American debut of Béla Bartók, the premiere of Aaron Copland's *Appalachian Spring* by the Martha Graham Company in 1944, among dozens of others. These archival broadcasts have been aired by networks in France, Italy, Australia, New Zealand, Bulgaria, and the former Soviet Union.

RECORDINGS

Recordings are becoming an increasingly important element in the Music Division's public programs; four separate series are now being produced. *Our Musical Past* features reissues of Karl Krueger's recordings of American orches-

The Beaux Arts Trio. Trio in Residence at the Library of Congress.

tral music, originally released by the Society for the Preservation of the American Musical Heritage; the repertoire highlights unusual or lesser-known works: nineteenth-century brass band music, conducted by Frederick Fennell, William Grant Still's *Afro-American Symphony,* and the *Gaelic Symphony* of Mrs. H. H. A. Beach.

Chamber Music from the Library of Congress, distributed by Koch International, offers performances recorded in the Coolidge Auditorium by the American Chamber Players—a mixture of classic and modern works, including John Harbison's

Twilight Music, for horn, violin, and piano, and the two piano quintets of Ernest Bloch. *Classic Performances* spotlights the Music Division's concert archives, with legendary performances by such artists as African-American soprano Dorothy Maynor, Leopold Stokowski and The Symphony of the Air, and Zino Francescatti performing with Robert Casadesus.

The Music Division is a collaborator in The Leonore Gershwin/Library of Congress Recording and Publishing Project, a new series of recordings of vintage musicals by George and Ira Gershwin, produced by Elektra-Nonesuch and Roxbury Recordings, established by Leonore Gershwin. *Girl Crazy, Strike Up the Band, Lady, Be Good!,* and *Pardon My English* have been carefully restored using original sources in the Division's collections; performers for these recordings are specialists in the musical styles of the Gershwin era. New recordings of works commissioned by the Library of Congress also receive support from the McKim Fund and other Library foundations.

PUBLICATIONS

Publications issued by the Music Division include facsimile reproductions of important manuscripts in its collections: the Brahms *Violin Concerto;* the Mozart *Gran Partita,* K.361 *(Serenade for 13 Instruments);* and the Mendelssohn *Octet.* The most recent facsimile, "Johannes Brahms: Three Lieder on Poems of Adolf Friedrich von Schack," was published in 1983, commemorating the 150th anniversary of the composer's birth—part of a celebration that included an international Brahms Conference and Festival. Other publications include bibliographies *(The Music Manuscripts, First Editions, and Correspondence of Franz Liszt in the Collections of the Music Division, Library of Congress),* and Louis Charles Elson lectures given by some of the world's leading musical scholars—Karl Geiringer, Jacques Barzun, Jaap Kunst, Donald Grout, and Egon Wellesz, among others.

Foundations such as the Coolidge, Elson, Moldenhauer, Sonneck, and Whittall support the publication of scholarly books, monographs, editions, and essays. Recent publications of this nature include *Brahms Studies: Analytical and Historical Perspectives: Papers Delivered at the International Brahms Conference, Washington, D.C., May 1983* (Oxford University Press); *The Complete Works of William Billings* (The American Musicological Society and the Colonial Society of Massachusetts); *A Celebration of American Music: Words and Music in Honor of H. Wiley Hitchcock* (University of Michigan Press); and *American Sacred Music Imprints, 1698–1810: A Bibliography* (American Antiquarian Society).

Music Division publications.
(Photograph by Jim Higgins)

The Music
of Americans

THE LIBRARY OF CONGRESS has perhaps the strongest collection of popular music of any library in the world. It has sheet music for standards ("Someone to Watch over Me"), for tunes so well-known it is hard to imagine them as notes-on-paper ("My Melancholy Baby"), and for thousands of songs that hoped for popularity in vain—"popular" in style, unpopular in fact. Most important to the researcher, it has the many tunes that were once popular and are now little-known. These tunes may be important for conjuring up a time, understanding a reference in a novel (it was in the Music Division that "Seaside Girls," the song Leopold Bloom remembers obsessively in his wanderings around Dublin, in James Joyce's *Ulysses*, was first found), or documenting the use of a word (the *Oxford English Dictionary* lists the song "Mr. Jefferson Lord, Play that Barber Shop Chord" as the first use of "barbershop" for a style of harmony).

The Music Division's collection of American popular music is strong from the beginnings (whatever you may define those beginnings to be); for European and Latin American popular music its collection is strong from the 1920s on. Thus, if you are interested in what Josephine Baker sang in Paris—or Charles Trenet, or Jacques Brel—the Library of Congress is your best American source; if you want to find the kind of dance-band arrangements that were really played at the Berlin cabarets between the wars, they are at the Music Division, too. Or if you are interested in the Cuban *conjunto* music which forms the basis of Oscar Hijuelos's *The Mambo Kings Play Songs of Love*, you will find much of it—ready to slap on the stands and play—in the Music Division.

Because publishers wanted to get music into the Copyright Office as soon as possible, the Music Division has many popular songs in versions which differ from the standard published versions. Often this is disappointing: a handsome song cover that is prized by collectors will not be present in the Library's copy, which will contain either the music only, or the music enclosed in a drab cover listing "Most Recent Instrumental and Vocal Successes." But sometimes these different versions are fascinating and very rare: the songs from *Oklahoma!*, for instance, in a cover bearing the show's earlier name *Away We Go.* "My Old Flame" in a cover with Mae West smiling out, advertising her new picture as *It Ain't No Sin.* (The title was changed to *Belle of the Nineties.*) Occasionally you can see a popular song taking shape before your eyes. Take, for example, "Sleepy Time Gal," one of those songs so well-known it is hard to imagine them being published. We have the published version, but we also have the first, unpublished copyright of the song. Both versions are about a girl who stays up all night dancing, but

George M. Cohan, William Jerome, and Jean Schwartz. *Take Your Girl to the Ball Game.* New York: Cohan & Harris, 1908. Attempting to capitalize on the success of *Take Me out to the Ball Game* in 1908, many composers wrote songs glamorizing baseball in the early 1900s.

Harrigan and Hart's Patrick's Day Parade Songster. New York: A. J. Fisher, 1847. The "songster," which contained words, but not music, to a collection of currently popular songs, was a common way of selling such songs to an audience which could not read musical notation.

the endings are utterly different. In the published version, the singer looks for the time when the girl will change:

> *You'll learn to cook and to sew,*
> *What's more you'll love it I know*
> *When you're a stay-at-home,*
> *Play-at-home,*
> *Eight o'clock sleepy-time gal.*

But the singer of the first version wants the girl to stay as she is:

> *The music has played*
> *Because it's you who has stayed*
> *My wonderful,*
> *Wide-awake,*
> *Dreamy-eyed sleepy-time gal.*

All this is published music. The Music Division has popular music also in manuscript form. Much of it came in through copyright—occasionally in the hand of a major musician. (When a researcher called up the copyright for Louis Armstrong's "Gully Low Blues" he found that it was in Armstrong's hand.)

Much of the sound of American popular music is tied up with the dance orchestras that played it. The Music Division has a large collection of published "stocks"—sets of parts for dance orchestras. It also has Ferde Grofé's own library of parts for his dance orchestra, containing many arrangements in the hand of the writer of the *Grand Canyon Suite* as well as many commercial "stocks" which Grofé has altered for his orchestra.

Harry von Tilzer, writer of many turn-of-the-century hits ("A Bird in a Gilded Cage," "On a Sunday Afternoon," "Down Where the Wurzburger Flows," "Wait 'Til the Sun Shines, Nellie"), founded his own music publishing firm shortly after 1900. It published his own songs, along with such other hits as "Row, Row, Row." The Music Division has the papers of the firm, which give a glimpse of the business life of Tin Pan Alley at the beginning of the present century.

American popular music is intimately tied up with American musical theater. The Music Division has one of the great collections of published music from the American musical theater; it also is the repository of the manuscripts of many of America's show composers. The list includes:

The National Negro Opera Company performing Robert Nathaniel Dett's *The Ordering of Moses* at Griffith Stadium, Washington, D.C., on July 28, 1950. *(National Negro Opera Company Collection)*

JOHN PHILIP SOUSA: Now thought of primarily as "The March King," Sousa was known during his lifetime also for his rollicking operettas. Venturesome repertory companies still revive his *El Capitan,* a tale of South American politicking, whose tunes are the source of the march of the same name.

VICTOR HERBERT, writer of "Ah, Sweet Mystery of Life," "I'm Falling in Love with Someone," "Indian Summer," and "Kiss Me Again." Herbert tried his hand at all sorts of music: there are overtures for silent films, ballets written for interpolation in Ziegfeld *Follies,* two full-scale cello concertos—even a full-length hiss-the-villain silent movie score. Even for shows you thought you knew there are surprises: the manuscript of *Babes in Toyland* starts with a ten-minute orchestral storm-at-sea—not in the published vocal score—that was supposed to do the same thing for the plot of *Babes in Toyland* that the tornado did for the 1903 stage show *The Wizard of Oz.*

IRVING BERLIN: The papers of the man whom Jerome Kern said "IS American popular music," including material from shows from *Watch Your Step* (1916; its big hit was "Play a Simple Melody") to *Mr. President* (1962). Irving Berlin did not himself write notes on paper, so there are no "Irving Berlin music manuscripts"; there is, however, a variety of performance material, documenting some shows, including *Annie Get Your Gun,* in extreme detail. And there are fascinating sketches of the lyrics to Berlin songs, including revisions and extra verses. Here, for example, is a version of "There's No Business Like Show Business" written for Mary Martin when she played Dallas, Texas, in 1955:

Asleep AT THE Switch

by CHARLES SHACKFORD

CHICAGO, ILL. PUBLISHED E.T. PAULL MUSIC CO. 20 EAST LONDON ENG.
LYON & HEALY BY 17TH ST. HOWARD & CO.

NEW YORK

CHICAGO, ILL. TORONTO, CAN. CINCINNATI & CHICAGO
NATIONAL MUSIC CO. WHALEY ROYCE & CO. THE JOHN CHURCH CO.
COPYRIGHT 1897 BY E.T. PAULL The Gillin Printing Co. N.Y.

... no business I know.
Playing Broadway at the famous Palace
Don't compare with this, it's simply grand.
Ask me how I feel to be in Dallas;
Like little Alice
In Wonderland.
There's no people like show people,
They smile when they are low.
Who'd have thought when I was on my mother's knee
I'd be in Texas? But here I be
Gettin' paid for doin' what comes natur'lly:
Let's go on with the show.

VINCENT YOUMANS: The Music Division has the largest collection of the manuscripts of Vincent Youmans, the composer of such shows as *Hit the Deck!* and *Great Day.* Save perhaps for *No, No, Nanette,* the shows themselves are not much performed now, but the songs remain standards of the pop and jazz-singer repertories: "I Want to Be Happy," "Flying Down to Rio," "Without a Song," "Hallelujah!," "Sometimes I'm Happy," "Time on My Hands," and even that standby of standbys for tap dancers, "Tea for Two."

GEORGE GERSHWIN: In addition to the manuscripts of Gershwin's concert works, the Gershwin Collection has considerable manuscript music for his stage musicals—especially *Of Thee I Sing* ("Love Is Sweeping the Country") and *Let 'Em Eat Cake* ("Mine"). It also has material from his late songs for Hollywood musicals, with Gershwin's own piano accompaniments crafted carefully as an art song: "They Can't Take That away from Me," "Nice Work if You Can Get It," "Slap That Bass." The Division has full score, sketch score, typescript libretto, and sheaves of sketches for the archetypal American opera, *Porgy and Bess.* The Collection also contains material concerning Ira Gershwin, including letters to Ira from Kurt Weill written during their collaboration on *Lady in the Dark.*

RICHARD RODGERS is represented in several collections. The Richard Rodgers Collection contains his own sketches for his songs; the Oscar Hammerstein Collection contains correspondence, programs, sketches, and miscellaneous material from the Rodgers and Hammerstein era. Robert Russell Bennett's orchestrator's scores for several of the Rodgers and Hammerstein shows are within the Richard Rodgers Collection, as well.

LEONARD BERNSTEIN: The Music Division has holograph versions of songs

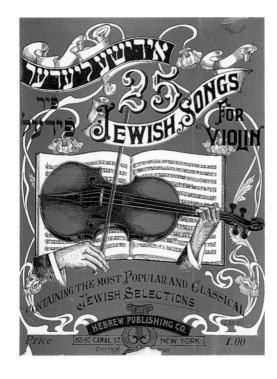

ABOVE. *Jewish Songs for Violin: Containing the Most Popular and Classial Jewish Selections.* New York: Hebrew Publishing Co., 1910.

OPPOSITE. Charles Shackford, music and lyrics. *Asleep at the Switch.* New York: E. T. Paull Music Co., 1897. No publisher of popular music undertood better than E. T. Paull that elaborate covers sold sheet music. *Asleep at the Switch,* with its soft-focus cover art, is subtle for Paull—in comparison to the strongly delineated designs and colors that give full impact to such Paull stalwarts as *The Burning of Rome, The Ben-Hur Chariot Race,* and *Napoleon's Last Charge.*

from *On the Town*, *Wonderful Town*, *Candide*, *Peter Pan*, and *West Side Story*. Some of this material shows music we know well in earlier guises. Larry Kert, who created the role of Tony in *West Side Story*, remembers of the first version of the Balcony Scene:

At that time, it was a twelve-minute scene; there was so much glorious music in it. But, for the-atrical reasons, much of the music was cut and it emerged a seven-minute scene.

It is the earlier, twelve-minute scene that is present in the manuscripts.

The music of black Americans comes in a rainbow of colors. The immemorial spirituals show up in the Music Division in early Civil War publications, in the many editions of the Fisk Jubilee Singers' biography and souvenir books, in other collections of Jubilee singers before the turn of the century, and in many twentieth-century versions. These versions from our century include arrangements for voice and piano, the choral arrangements through which many of these spirituals are best known today, and new-wave collections like *Ain't You Got a Right to the Tree of Life*, done with the aid of tape recorders, which try to fix in notation just how the folk from whom the spirituals were collected actually sang them.

Secular black music in the Division goes back as far as dances played by Francis Johnson's famous band of free blacks, which was the toast of Philadelphia early in the nineteenth century. The sounds of his band are forever gone, since we have the music only in the form of piano arrangements; but the toe-tapping tunes still remain. There is a great deal of music from the early minstrel stage, challenging the researcher in black music to decide what is bona fide borrowing from black originals and what is just white folks' jokes. (What can we trust from *The Ethiopian Glee Book: A Collection of Popular Negro Melodies Arranged for Quartet Clubs* by "Gumbo Chaff…first banjo player to the King of Congo" [Boston: Howe, 1847]?)

African-American secular music speaks with its own voice in the rags which began to be published just before the turn of the century. The Music Division has all of Scott Joplin's rags in first edition, along with the rags of other pioneers of the genre—James Scott, Arthur Marshall, Joseph Lamb, and Artie Matthews.

As ragtime was starting its career, the black musical theater was beginning on Broadway. Shows with titles promising exotic locales—*A Trip to Coontown*, *In Dahomey*, *Bandana Land*—featured leading comics such as Bert Williams and George Walker and major singers such as Aida Overton Walker and Abbie Mitchell Cook (who was later to be the first to sing "Summertime" in *Porgy and Bess*).

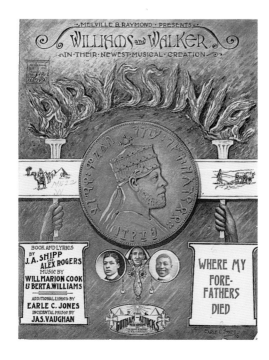

ABOVE. *Abyssinia*, with music by Will Marion Cook and lyrics by Alex Roger, was both written by, acted by, and published by African-Americans. The publishing house, Gotham-Attucks, was named, in part, for Crispus Attucks, black victim of the Boston Massacre.

OPPOSITE. Bert A. Williams, music and Alex Rogers, lyrics. *Let It Alone*. New York: Gotham-Attucks, 1906. Sung by Bert Williams, premier African-American entertainer of the first two decades of this century, the chorus of the song advises against meddling in other persons' affairs: "If it don't concern you … mind your own bus'ness and let it alone."

43

Naestsan Biyin: Song of the Earth. From the culture of the Navajo people, this Hozhonji Song, collected and transcribed by folklorist Natalie Curtis Burlin, is a benediction on the created world. It declares that, in nature, contrasting elements are complements and helpmates of one another: "Now the Mother Earth and the Father Sky, meeting, joining one another, helpmates ever, they. All is beautiful, indeed."

Songwriters for this theater included James Weldon Johnson (later Executive Secretary of the NAACP), J. Rosamond Johnson, and Will Marion Cook. Cook was among the first black Americans to have his songs published by a major American "legitimate" (as opposed to popular-song) publisher; the Johnson Brothers, with Bob Cole, were the first black song composers to be accepted as part of the standard popular-music scene, writing ballads for general singing ("The Maiden with the Dreamy Eyes") as well as racial material ("Under the Bamboo Tree"). This material is represented in the Music Division in myriad arrangements—song with piano, male quartet, mixed quartet, wind band, and potted-palm orchestra. There are even scripts for some of the shows—*Abyssinia, In Dahomey, Jes Lak White Folks,* and *The Cannibal King*—of which the first two are also represented in the sheet music published by Gotham-Attucks, the first successful black-owned music publishing firm. This firm, created in 1905 by the merger of the Gotham Music Publishing Company and the Attucks Music Publishing Company (the latter named for the black protomartyr of American freedom), also published such well-known songs as "Nobody," Bert Williams's trademark song, and the jazz standard "Shine." Later black-owned music companies such as Handy Bros. and Jobete—the latter the publishing arm of Motown Records—are also well-represented in the Music Division's collections.

The great monuments of jazz are generally considered to be recordings—located in the Recorded Sound Reference Center of the Library rather than the Music Division. Nonetheless, the paper trail of jazz is substantial. Books and periodicals on jazz and jazzmen are published in many languages (*Jazznytt,* a periodical published in Stockholm; *Cutia de Rezonanţa: Eseuri despre Jazz din Perspectiva Culturii Actuale,* a book published in Bucharest in 1985). Discographies document the work of most major performers, and one epic forty-volume discography tries to document every jazz recording through 1967.

Jazz is finally represented by notes on paper as well. Many standard pieces were published in "stock" arrangements, sets of parts for bands to play. The Library has a wide if somewhat haphazard selection of such "stocks," not all of which were deposited for copyright. With them your band can attempt such standards as Jelly Roll Morton's "Milenburg Joys," King Oliver's "Sugar Foot Stomp," Earl Hines's "Salt Peanuts," and a whole bunch of Basie, ranging al-

LEFT. N. P. Beers and M. Colburn. *Rising of the People: The DrumTap Rattles Through the Land. Patriotic Song.* New York: Firth, Pond & Co., 1862. Crowded with symbols of northern patriotism, this sheet-music cover was clearly designed by its publisher to appeal to staunch supporters of the Union cause.

RIGHT. J. P. Webster, music and Rev. H. D. L. Webster, lyrics. *Lorena.* Chicago: H. M. Higgins, 1857, 1861. Civil War diarist Mary Boykin Chestnut wrote: "Maggie Howell (the sister-in-law of President Jefferson Davis), says there is a girl in large hoops and a calico frock at every piano between Richmond and Mississippi, banging on the out of tune thing and looking up into a man's face, singing that song. The man wears a soiled and battle stained uniform, but his heart is fresh enough, as he hangs over her, to believe in Lorena."

phabetically from "Aces and Faces" to "Wiggle Woogie," and including such standards as "One O'clock Jump." Combo players can try their hand at Lionel Hampton's "Hamp's Boogie Woogie" or Charlie Parker's "Scrapple from the Apple: featuring the original Charlie Parker Alto Sax Solo."

More and more as the century wore on, black composers wrote for the concert hall. The Music Division has manuscripts of music by the pioneers of this group, including the seminal *Afro-American Symphony* of William Grant Still. (It also has Still's letters to the dedicatee of the symphony, Irving Schwerké.) It has the manuscript of the "Rhapsodie Negre" of Florence Price, the first black woman to write a symphony performed by a major orchestra: the Music Division's photostat of Price's piano sonata, deposited for copyright, is the only known copy of this piece, which is now becoming something of a repertory work for pianists interested in African-American music. The Music Division also holds a large number of manuscripts of Ulysses Kay, and manuscripts of representative recent composers such as David Baker and Jeffrey Mumford.

As black composers made a bid for entry into the mainstream of American concert life, so did black performers. One of the symbols of this movement was the National Negro Opera Company, active between 1943 and 1962. The Music Division has programs, photographs, and papers of the NNOC.

A new kind of black sacred music, usually called "gospel" (as is another kind of music most often done by white performers), developed in the twentieth century. During its early years it was little-recorded, and songs in this style spread largely through printed copies. The Library of Congress is the only major music library to have an important collection of the early publications of such pioneering gospel companies as Martin & Akers. It has copies of the original editions of such gospel standards as "99½ Won't Do," "God Specializes," "Take Your Burden to the Lord and Leave It There," and that arch-symbol of gospel, "Take My Hand, Precious Lord."

As other ethnic strains in American popular music become of interest, other sections of the Music Division's collections will be reappraised: Yiddish theater music published on the East Side of New York; Czech polkas published in Chicago; Italian band music published in Brooklyn; German male-chorus (Männerchor) music published in the Midwest; Latin-American popular music published right by Tin Pan Alley; the music of the village-green band published (and in manuscript) from New England to Oskaloosa, Iowa. If it was a music which people enjoyed enough to have it published, chances are it can be found in the Music Division.

Duke Ellington performing at the Hurricane Club in New York. Ellington is stopping his ears in order to hear the band more clearly above the ambient noise of the club. *(Prints and Photographs Division) (Photograph by Gordon Parks)*

The Theater

APRIMARY HALLMARK OF THE WORLD OF THE THEATER is its astonishing variety: it encompasses a vast array of performance genres and production circumstances. Virtually all of these are reflected, often in considerable abundance, in the theater collections of the Library of Congress. Various elements of these collections will be found in several of the reading rooms of the Library, their location generally determined by the kind or type of material in question. In these reading rooms, scholars and artists have worked long hours pursuing projects directed toward reconstruction of various noteworthy performance events from the nation's theatrical past, perhaps for scholarly, or perhaps for actual new production purposes. Because of the enormity of the Library's theater collections, the staff has grown accustomed to hearing that someone has "discovered," in a Library collection, a stage script, for example, previously thought lost.

The scope of these collections includes books, periodicals, playbills, manuscripts, letters, promptbooks, production photographs, and scenic design. The sheer magnitude of elements in the collections endow the Library with certain special strengths without parallel in other libraries. Its published and unpublished stage scripts, for example, give the Library the largest collection of American drama in the world.

One of the nation's major theater resources is the Library's collection of unpublished dramas deposited for copyright since 1870—in itself a formidable basis for the study of American theatrical, social, cultural, and literary history. Here, a reader can find scripts from American musical comedy, burlesque, the legitimate stage, and vaudeville, much of which would have been lost had it not been for copyright deposit. Thanks to a law protecting a writer's work from unauthorized use, the public can inquire into aspects of our nation's fabulous stage history to an extent not possible anywhere else.

The Library's Rare Book and Special Collections Division holds a number of notable collections of published drama. The Raymond Toinet Collection of French literature contains a significant number of editions of plays, primarily of the seventeenth and early eighteenth centuries. The Francis Longe Collection of theater works published in English between 1607 and 1812 includes original plays, theatrical adaptations, and translations credited to over six hundred playwrights, and is particularly rich in the works of lesser-known seventeenth-century figures. Particularly prized in the Division are copies of the 1599 Quarto edition of Shakespeare's *Romeo and Juliet*, the First Folio edition (1623), the Quarto edition (1619) of *Midsummer Night's Dream*, and copies of the 1632, 1664, and 1685 folios.

Frank Wedekind. Stock lithograph poster for the *Ibsen Theater*, Vienna, early June 1898, with autograph manuscript of the first draft of the prologue to the drama *Erdgeist* on verso. Wedekind created this additional material when he was told that the Viennese public would not understand his play without a prologue. Later, it became the famous opening of Alban Berg's opera, *Lulu*. (*Moldenhauer Archives in the Library of Congress*)

ABOVE. Water color and ink costume design by Lucinda Ballard for the 1946 revival of Jerome Kern and Oscar Hammerstein II's *Show Boat. (Oscar Hammerstein II Collection)*

OPPOSITE. Ladies of the Opera. From the lower left-hand corner, clockwise: Amelita Galli-Curci, Rise Stevens, Lily Pons, Rosa Ponselle, Inge Borkh. In the center: Frances Alda *(Charles Jahant Collection)*

The Roman playwrights Terence and Plautus are represented in several incunabula. Among the editions of Terence are four copies of a Strasbourg incunabulum of 1496, particularly important for the history of theater production for woodcuts believed to be among the first representations of performance of Terence on the Renaissance stage. The Division also holds a copy of a German translation of 1486 of Terence's *Eunuchus,* four copies of the Aldine Aristophanes of 1498, and a Plautus manuscript of eighty-seven leaves dated 1487 containing eight of his plays.

The Library's coverage of both classic and contemporary Asian drama is remarkable. The Asian Division's collection of original Chinese-language plays is extensive, probably the largest outside China. Its collection of Japanese plays is likely the largest outside Japan, and it is comprehensive in the coverage of Nō, Kabuki, and Kyogen titles.

The Library's theatrical manuscript collections include papers of prominent persons from virtually all professions in theater: composers, actors, directors, producers, writers, and variety artists. The Library's Manuscript Division is particularly rich in papers of women prominent in the American theater, some of whom were also active abroad. Laura Keene and Charlotte Cushman were actress-managers whose papers offer invaluable insights into the business of the stage in the nineteenth century. Minnie Maddern Fiske possessed an extraordinary intellect with which she forged new levels of realism on the American stage. Margaret Webster directed highly acclaimed operatic and Shakespearean productions. Ruth Gordon's papers include her business correspondence, production material, programs, and general business papers from Thornton Wilder's *The Matchmaker* and other plays.

Located primarily in the Music Division, the Library's lyric stage collections are another of its special strengths, affording the researcher perhaps the single most important and powerful resource to be found anywhere for the study of American musical theater. Many of these collections contain significant quantities of stage production and business material, in addition to a wealth of musical scores.

In the Irving Berlin Collection are scripts, posters and theater programs, song books, lyric sheets, sheet music, photographs, and considerable business material, including documentation on the Music Box Theater in New York City, a theater which Berlin owned originally with producer Sam Harris. The George and Ira Gershwin Collection is the largest public collection of original source materials for the study of the work and life of the Gershwins. It includes virtu-

Richard Rodgers (seated at piano) and
Oscar Hammerstein II. *(Richard Rodgers
Collectrion)*

ally all of the major Gershwin works in autograph manuscript, as well as autograph music sketches and scores, scrapbooks, financial records, contracts, correspondence, telegrams, and scripts for Gershwin stage and film productions.
There is material on the Gershwins' relations with the Theatre Guild, the original producer of *Porgy and Bess;* with Alex Aarons and Vinton Freedley, producers of many Gershwin musicals; with the Shubert organization; and with Florenz Ziegfeld for whom the Gershwins began work on the show, *East Is West,*
which never finally materialized. There is correspondence from George White,

producer of the *Scandals* revue series, to George Gershwin, and there are copies of contracts for such Ira Gershwin shows as Kurt Weill's *Firebrand of Florence.*

The Oscar Hammerstein II Collection covers his early musicals, for which he wrote both "book" and lyrics, as well as his later collaborations with Richard Rodgers. The collection contains scripts, notes, librettos, correspondence, printed music, pictorial materials, playbills from a variety of places, and awards. *Oklahoma!* and *South Pacific* are particularly well documented. The *South Pacific* folder includes material on lighting arrangements, tour scheduling, casting, contracts, program creation, and record album matters. The *Pipe Dream* folder includes illustrations for set designs by Jo Mielziner for the show. Scrapbooks include many production photographs of various shows with which Hammerstein was connected.

The David Merrick Collection covers the greatest part of the career of a man recognized as one of the most prominent producers of our day. It includes a large number of promptbooks containing script, lighting, and other stage cues, property lists, notes on costuming, and other production-related material. Productions covered include *How Now, Dow Jones* with score by Elmer Bernstein, *110 in the Shade* of Tom Jones and Harvey Schmidt, and *Take Me Along* and *Carnival,* with music and lyrics by Robert Merrill. Also in the collection are early drafts of *Funny Girl, Child's Play,* and *The Rothschilds.* Performance materials in the Merrick Collection which complement composers' holographs found elsewhere in the Music Division derive from Harold Rome's *Fanny* and *I Can Get It for You Wholesale,* and *Breakfast at Tiffany's,* with music and lyrics by Robert Merrill.

Of particular interest among the materials in the Moldenhauer Archives at the Library of Congress is the autograph copy of the celebrated prologue to Frank Wedekind's once highly controversial play, *Erdgeist.* It is written on the back of a copy of the poster used for a tour in 1898 through Germany and Austria-Hungary of the theater company Ibsen Theater, which was presenting *Erdgeist* in repertory. According to period documentation, when the company was about to present *Erdgeist* in Vienna, the company director, Carl Heine, told Wedekind that the Viennese public would not understand the play without an explanatory prologue, and in response Wedekind, then and there, wrote the requisite addition on the poster.

The Prints and Photographs Division has custody of the vast majority of the Library's theater iconography. In its remarkable performing arts poster collection are 5,000 nineteenth-century lithographs, chromolithographs, and woodcuts pertaining to circus, rodeo, minstrelsy, specialty acts, burlesque, magic, vaudeville, opera, operetta, and theater. Ranging in size from small window cards to immense

ABOVE LEFT. Florenz Ziegfeld discovered Kathleen Rose in a New York City dress salon where she worked as a model. Always known simply as "Dolores," she became one of the most famous of Ziegfeld's show girls, appearing in editions of his *Follies* and *Midnight Frolics.* She is one of many Ziegfeld girls photographed by Alfred Cheney Johnston. This photograph is particularly significant as a record of a spectacular design. It was in the *Frolics* that Dolores wore this white satin costume with pearls and an enormous fan towering over her statuesque figure. (*Alfred Cheney Johnston Collection, Prints and Photographs Division*)

multiple-sheet posters, these works constitute a panorama of American theater during the later nineteeth century and include many brilliantly colored illustrations of spectacles, legitimate drama, and a large number of poster advertisements for the leading minstrel groups of the time. American theater in the earlier nineteenth century is well documented through prints from engravers and lithographers of the period, of whom Currier & Ives and Thomas & Wylie were the most prominent.

Minnie Maddern Fiske's photographic collection is the Library's largest photographic record of any single actor, with studio portraits of Mrs. Fiske, scenes from many of her plays and the plays of contemporaries such as George Arliss and Otis Skinner, and photographs used in designing stage sets.

The Division's theater photographs include original daguerreotypes from the middle of the nineteenth century of Jenny Lind and Junius Brutus Booth and original Mathew Brady glass plate negatives. There is an exceedingly large number of portraits of theater personalities by noted theatrical photographers such as Napoleon Sarony, Aimée Dupont, Joseph Byron, Otto Sarony, B. J. Falk, and Arnold Genthe. Alfred Cheney Johnston's photographs of numerous Ziegfeld girls and prominent New York musical comedy personalities are an invaluable record of earlier twentieth-century American variety theater.

This brief space can afford only an overview of a theater collection that certainly can lay claim to being one of the finest of its kind, a collection in which the Library and the nation can take pride.

Faust. Theater poster. Lewis Morrison was one of the more popular American actors of the later nineteenth century. His production of *Faust* in the 1880s reflects a theatrical fashion of the time. Gounod's version of *Faust* opened the Metropolitan Opera House in 1883, and Henry Irving appeared in W. G. Will's adaptation in 1887 with George Alexander and Ellen Terry. *(Prints and Photographs Division)*

OPPOSITE RIGHT. *The War of Wealth: Run on the Bank.* Theater poster. Opening in New York City on February 10, 1896, *The War of Wealth* was one of several melodramas with popular appeal written by Charles Turner Dazey. His most successful effort was *In Old Kentucky* of 1893. *(Prints and Photographs Division)*

Invitation
to the Dance

Léon Bakst. Costume design for the ballet *Sleeping Princess.* Watercolor and ink. Bakst designed the costumes and decor for this production; first performed by the Ballets Russes in London at the Alhambra Theatre, on November 2, 1921. The Music Division acquired this drawing in 1984 from the collection of dancer, choreographer, and ballet master Serge Lifar. *(Prints and Photographs Division)*

Resources for the study of dance have always had a place at the Library of Congress. This long-term commitment is evidenced by the early acquisition of eighteenth- and nineteenth-century dance manuals. Dance materials at the Library serve as a mirror to the interest in—and commitment to—dance as an intrinsic component of the nation's cultural tapestry.

During the eighteenth and nineteenth centuries America was a country isolated by region and largely rural; American dancing of this period was, to a great degree, centered in the home and community, not the theater or music hall. This tradition is reflected in the Library's superb collection of eighteenth- and nineteenth-century dance manuals. Such guidebooks were used by the traveling "dancing masters," circuit-riders of the era who traversed vast regions of the United States teaching dances to the gentry of the South and the middle and upper classes of the Northeast. These dancing masters used manuals published in Europe and the British Isles, and the Library has numerous superb examples of these publications in the Music Division. Several examples include Pierre Landrin's *Potpourri françois de contre-dance ancienne* (Paris, 1760); P. Valleau Cartier, *Cartier's Practical Illustrated Waltz Instructor, Ball-room Guide and Call Book* (New York, 1880); C. J. von Feldtenstein's *Erweiterung der Kunst nach der Choreographie zu tanzen, Tänze zu erfinden,...* (Braunschweig, 1772); and James P. Cassidy's *Treatise on the Theory and Practice of Dancing* (Dublin, 1810).

During the nineteenth century the scholarly study of dancing was limited, and the Library's collections are reflective of this fact. With the arrival of the twentieth century and the development of such fields as anthropology and folklore, however, scholars in these newly created disciplines began to study the dance and other expressive elements of cultural groups represented both in America and throughout the world. This new scholarship, including histories written during the same period, provides rich sources of dance-related materials. Extremely numerous and important examples of anthropological data can be found in the Margaret Mead Collection, located in the Manuscript Division. Particularly rich dance items are among the Pacific Ethnographic Archives (one part of the Mead Collection). Examples include photographs from the field work conducted by Margaret Mead, Gregory Bateson, and others during the 1930s in Bali and New Guinea, and photographs taken by Colin McPhee and Jane Belo for their own research and then acquired by Mead.

Besides the acquisition of scholarly books and monographs, the Library plays an active part in the development of new scholarship in the field of folklore through its Archive of Folk Culture and the American Folklife Center.

Originally a section of the Music Division, the Archive (then called the Archive of Folk Song) carries out extensive field trips collecting and recording folk music (and related materials) throughout the United States. Field research began in 1928 and continues to the present day. Primary documentation and description of American vernacular dance exists in the Archive's collections. Recordings and other documents from Library projects are used by patrons through the Archive of Folk Culture's reading room in the Jefferson Building, and the Recorded Sound Reference Center, Motion Picture, Broadcasting, and Recorded Sound Division, in the Performing Arts Reading Room in the Madison Building.

Due to its ephemeral nature, theatrical dance in America has been poorly documented, and until recently the art was not treated seriously as a potential area of scholarly inquiry. This state of affairs has left libraries and archives with documents that have been preserved by virtue of their relationship to another field, such as music, theater, or cultural history. Examples of materials of this type are dancing and dancers depicted on sheet music covers. These lithographs offer dance researchers of today a glimpse of what specific dances may have looked like, including the costuming of the period. Many of these pieces of sheet music include textual descriptions of the steps to these dances.

Documentation of such masterpieces as the Library's commission of Aaron Copland and Martha Graham's *Appalachian Spring* exists for today's scholars and performers to study only because the dance commission was linked to the musical commission. At the time *Appalachian Spring* was created in 1944, the Graham materials were preserved because they documented the Coolidge commission, not because of any intentional effort to document dance. Other examples of this passive—but, in hindsight, critically important—dance collecting include the dance photographs of Arnold Genthe housed in the Prints and Photographs Division. Genthe, a master photographer of the early twentieth century, became famous for his impressionistic portrayals of society women, artists, dancers, and theater personalities. The Library acquired the major portion of Genthe's studio archives shortly after his death in 1942.

In the early years of this century there was an explosion of creative energy in theatrical dance. The Ballets Russes of Sergei Diaghilev was at the very core of this explosion and was perhaps the most important theatrical dance phenomenon of the first twenty-five years of the twentieth century. Much documentation of this group has been preserved, and the Music Division is proud to own the music library of Diaghilev and the personal "notebook" from his last years. These

ABOVE. Franziska Boas and unidentified dancer in her *Dance Drama.* The Library's collection of Boas materials documents the many dimensions of Boas' career as a dancer, educator, and social activist. *(Franziska Boas Collection) (Photograph by P. A. Dearborn)*

OPPOSITE. Gwen Verdon. In 1956, Miss Verdon won the Tony Award for "Best Actress in a Musical" for her portrayal of Lola in *Damn Yankees.* Bob Fosse, for his work in the same musical, received a Tony for "Best Choreography." *(Fosse-Verdon collection) (Photograph by Ormond Gigli)*

Isadora Duncan. This photograph is from a series of studies made by Arnold Genthe during 1915–1918, while Duncan was on tour in the United States. Famous for his impressionistic portraits of society women, artists, and theater personalities, Genthe's photos of dancers are among his best-known works. (*Arnold Genthe Collection, Prints and Photographs Division*)

extraordinary items are complemented by visual materials (a poster, a costume design, and a watercolor portrait of Nijinsky in *Les Orientales*) in the Prints and Photograph Division.

The most important event influencing the Library's resources in dance was the invention of motion pictures. For the first time, film made it possible to capture fully the dancer's image and, consequently, film profoundly changed the nature of dance documentation and scholarship. Because dance "moves," filmmakers—later, television producers—have been drawn to the dancing image since the very beginning of the film era, and dance scholars, seeing the tremendous potential for capturing the dance, immediately began to exploit film as a medium for enriching research resources. The results of this technological breakthrough are a vast motion picture collection in which dance is prominent. Dancing included in feature films has even become a major component of anthologies of the movies, such as *That's Entertainment* and *That's Dancing*. The Motion Picture, Broadcasting, and Recorded Sound Division has taken a leading role in the documentation and preservation of dance through its film collections. A reference book, *Guide to Dance in Film*, edited by David Parker of that Division, is the standard source for this area of dance study.

The development of low-cost videotape as a means to record dance has likewise produced major changes in the field of dance research. Creators of dance can now record dance quickly and easily; this is as true for vernacular dance practitioners as it is for theatrical dance. The result is an exciting new library of dance literature awaiting study and analysis. The Library's acquisition of such videotape material has been enormously enhanced by the revision of the copyright law (1976) that provides for the copyright registration of choreographic works. Consequently, the Library has received thousands of dance videotapes as a result of this provision. Examples include numerous deposits from George Balanchine (including: *Square Dance*, *Chaconne*, and *Stars and Stripes*) and Agnes de Mille (including *The Bitter Weird*, *Bloomer Girl*, and *Conversations About the Dance*).

The technology of film and video has wrought a dramatic change in the expectations and art of dance creators. Choreographers are able to know that their work will become an important part of artistic history long after they cease creating and dancing. This realization has spurred the Library's increased interest in preserving all aspects of dancers' and choreographers' creative work. Such new awareness of historical perspective has been an important tool for the acquisition of dance collections at the Library.

Bob Fosse directing Liza Minelli in the filming of *Cabaret*. *(Fosse-Verdon Collection)* *(Photograph by Lars Looschen)*

During the past fifty years choreographers and dancers have created and maintained personal collections of extraordinary value. Among the most significant in the Library are the Bob Fosse/Gwen Verdon Collection, the Martha Graham Videotape Collection, the Graham materials in the Coolidge Collection, and the Franziska Boas Collection. While each of these collections demonstrates a very different approach to the art of dance, all share a dependence on the moving image as the prime document of the creative artist. The Fosse/Verdon Collection, in particular, is a comprehensive assemblage of the high achievements of both Fosse and Verdon. Through their lives we are able to construct a rich picture of the dancer's world on Broadway and in film. The paper, manuscript, and photographic components of these collections are served to scholars and artists in the Music Division, and the video, film, and audio materials are available in the Motion Picture, Broadcasting, and Recorded Sound Division.

The Collections of Musical Instruments

Instrument collecting in the Music Division began with the generosity of Mrs. Gertrude Clarke Whittall. Well known in Washington for the *soirées musicales* which occurred frequently in her home, and wishing to have her own quartet of well-matched stringed instruments, she enlisted the aid of famed violinist Louis Krasner, who was able to locate no fewer than five excellent instruments by Antonio Stradivari which she purchased in 1934 and 1935: the "Castelbarco" cello (1697); the "Cassavetti" viola (1727); and three violins, the "Ward" (1700), the "Castelbarco" (1699), and the "Betts" (1704). Five Tourte bows accompanied the instruments. Mrs. Whittall also provided an endowment to ensure professional in-house use of her instruments as well as other music making within the scope and traditions of the Music Division. In addition, her gift included funding for the construction of a pavilion to house and display her instruments: the Whittall Pavilion, which adjoins the Coolidge Auditorium, was completed in 1939.

What is now sometimes called the Cremonese Collection received its sixth instrument in 1938, when Mrs. Robert Somers Brookings of Washington, D.C., presented the Library with her husband's fine violin, the "Brookings" (1654) by Niccolò Amati. The seventh arrived in 1952 when the great Austrian musician, Fritz Kreisler—American by naturalization—presented the Library with his manuscripts and memorabilia, the half-size violin on which he began studies as a young child, a fine violin bow made by Hill & Son, London, and one of his greatest violins, the "Kreisler," by Giuseppe Guarneri (1733).

In the early nineteenth century, the Cremonese instruments at the Library all received the then-standard alterations designed to increase their volume to a level demanded by players, and expected by audiences. While of continuing interest to numerous violin makers, who are sometimes commissioned to build replicas of them, the Library's strings remain performance instruments and are well known for the extensive duty they have served here. The Budapest String Quartet was the first major ensemble selected to play four of the Stradivari instruments on a regular and long-term basis. In 1962, the Juilliard String Quartet was selected to continue that tradition and is still the ensemble which plays those instruments in the Coolidge Auditorium performance series.

The following collections are considered museum objects and comprise a unique museum element within the library community at large. Selected objects from these collections, which can safely sustain playing conditions, have been treated and used in performance for early music and other scholarly events which seemed worth the risks that might apply to such usage. In general, these collections are used mostly by visiting researchers and craftsmen for various publication and instrument replication projects.

Viola d'Amore, mid eighteenth century; and Viola da Gamba, early eighteenth century. The Viola d'Amore (literally "love viol," probably so named for its sweetness of tone), in the foreground, was used for chamber music and solo playing in the eighteenth century. In the German tradition, as shown here, it was strung with seven bowed and seven sympathetic strings. In the background can be seen part of the neck and elaborately carved peg-box of a Viola da Gamba (or bass viol) attributed to Pieter Rombouts of Amsterdam. Such viols were constructed in various sizes, and usually had six strings, with a seventh occasionally added (as in this example) to extend the lower range. *(H. Blackiston Wilkins Collection) (Photograph by Jim Higgins)*

THE WILKINS COLLECTION

The second instrument collection that came to the Library consists of six early stringed instruments donated in 1937 by Dr. H. Blaikiston Wilkins, the former Honorary Curator of the Cremonese Collection. The Wilkins Collection includes a pardessus de viole (five-string treble viol), by Louis Guersan, Paris (1749); a fourteen-string viola d'amore by an unknown German maker (second half of the eighteenth century); a twelve-string viola d'amore by Ferdinando Gagliano, Naples (1763); a seven-string bass viol attributed to Pieter Rombouts, Amsterdam (early eighteenth century); a quinton (a five-string combination of violin and treble viol) by François le Jeune, Paris (1760); and the remains of a late-seventeenth-century bass viol (possibly by Joachim Teilke, Hamburg) which was converted into a cello, probably early in the nineteenth century.

THE MILLER COLLECTION

The third instrument collection to arrive at the Library was included in a bequest from Dr. Dayton C. Miller (1866–1941), a well-known physicist and professor at the Cleveland Case School of Applied Science (now Case Western Reserve University). Dr. Miller was an avid amateur flutist, and over a sixty-year period he assembled the world's largest collection of flutes and flute-related materials.

In addition to over 1,600 instruments, the Miller Collection contains enormous library holdings, about 10,000 pieces of music and 3,000 books, some being editions not known to exist elsewhere. The Library materials also include many diverse documents such as patents in nearly all wind instrument categories, letters, portraits, photographs, bills, concert programs, extensive personal correspondence, articles, news clippings, and trade catalogs from nearly every wind instrument manufacturer who was active during Miller's lifetime.

Three-dimensional objects, prints, and other works of graphic art are also generously represented in the collection: they include over six hundred prints and engravings, three bronzes, and nearly sixty statuettes and figurines. Almost all feature representations of a flutist or player of pipes.

The instruments include flutes and other wind instruments from nearly all cultures of the world. They date from about 1100 BC to the 1970s and range from toys

Curator of Musical Instruments, Robert Sheldon, with one of seventeen early nineteenth-century crystal flutes by Claude Laurent, Paris, in the Dayton C. Miller Collection. *(Photograph by Reid Baker)*

Professor Dayton C. Miller in his home studio, Cleveland, Ohio, ca. 1935, with examples from his wind instrument collection, given to the Music Division in 1941. *(Dayton C. Miller Collection)*

and simple folk instruments to sophisticated and complex mechanical specimens intended for professional use. Materials range from clay, bone, and bamboo to jade, ivory, and gold. Other instruments include a dozen oboes, thirteen clarinets (one of ivory), three bassoons, several bagpipe chanters, diverse folk reed instruments, and piano rolls for electric and pneumatic instruments.

At least 460 European and American makers are represented. Highlights include forty flutes from the Munich workshop of Theobald Boehm, Rodolf Greve, and Carl Mendler; a late Beethoven-era Viennese English horn; recorders by Rippert, Bressan, and Hotteterre; an early eighteenth-century oboe by Hendrik Richters, Amsterdam; an early American clarinet by Samuel Graves, Winchester, N.H.; and a Quantz-model traverso once owned and used by King Frederick the Great of Prussia. The Miller Collection is also very strong in Native American instruments.

THE THAI COLLECTION

The fourth collection received at the Library was a presentation in 1960 from King Bhumibol Adulyadej of Thailand. It consists of ten elegantly crafted Siamese-style folk instruments including a pair of *ching* (finger cymbals), one *thon* and one *rammana* (small hand-played drums), two *khlui* (vertical flutes, small and

medium) with red and gold brocade covers, one *jakhe* (a three-string zither somewhat similar to the Japanese Koto) with a red and gold brocade cover, two *sq-u,* and two *sq duang,* the last four instruments being two forms of a two-string (one course) fiddle played in upright position. Each of the *sq u* and *sq duang* has a lacquered wooden case with blue plush lining, and the *ching, thon,* and *rammana* all share a fifth such case.

In 1982 the Music Division began its move from the Jefferson Building—the oldest in the Library complex—to the newest edifice, the James Madison Memorial Building. The new facility included in the basement a special high security vault for the musical instrument collections. It is environmentally well maintained and spacious enough to permit several visitors convenient but controlled access to the varied collections. The new installation also included funding for a full-time curator whose duties include making sure that the collections are accessible to visitors.

While this vault is fully adequate and one of the best museum storage facilities of its type, it is temporary. Renovations of the Jefferson Building include a permanent space for all of the musical instrument collections. It will be in the northwest corner of the ground floor, adjacent to the Coolidge Auditorium and Whittall Pavilion, and will include public exhibit areas, laboratory facilities, a curator's office within a study area, and a reference collection vault. About 40 percent of the instrument holdings will be on exhibit, and the Cremonese stringed instruments will be returned to their original wall exhibit cases in the Whittall Pavilion.

Admission to the instrument collections in the Madison Building or those stored in future Jefferson Building reference collections is by appointment. The handling or playing of any specimen is dependent on its condition and materials plus the reasons for the proposed usage. Qualified researchers, students, and performers have, through the Miller and other instrument collections in the Library, an extraordinary opportunity to learn more about the history and musical qualities of these unique instruments.

Three violins from a collection of seven Cremonese stringed instruments in the Music Division. Left to right: Niccolò Amati, 1654 (the "Brookings"); Antonio Stradivari, 1704 (the "Betts"); Giuseppe Guarneri (del Gesù), 1733 (the "Kreisler"). *(Photograph by Dane Penland)*

W. A. Mozart. Gran Partita, K.361/270a, autograph full orchestral score; and period instruments. More commonly known as *Serenade for Thirteen Instruments,* the Gran Partita is not an orchestral serenade but pure wind music. It is a "divertimento," but the instrumentation far exceeds that of the customary wind sextet or octet. In seven movements, the Partita was written in 1780/1781; at the time of the premier of *Idomeneo* in Munich, and the beginning of the composer's residence in Vienna. The instruments shown are of the type Mozart would have recognized. At top, from the R. E. Sheldon Collection, is a clarinet in A, ca. 1795–1810, signed, and probably made by German immigrant Jacob Anthony of Philadelphia. It is shown with mouthpiece reed upward, which is the reverse of modern practice. The three-keyed oboe carries the date of 1793, and is the work of Johann Gottfried Liebel of Adorf, Germany. The extra interchangeable top joints of varying length were used to cope with the diverse pitch standards in Europe at the time. This instrument is one of over 1,600 wind instruments in the Dayton C. Miller Collection at the Library of Congress. *(Photograph by Reid Baker)*

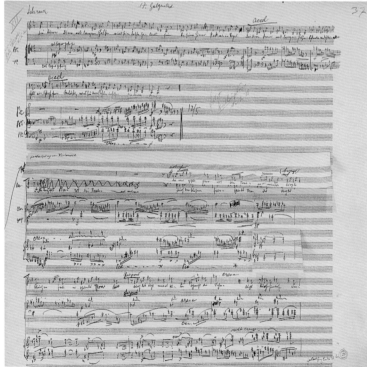

Service
to the Public
and to the
Collections

WHO USES THE MUSIC DIVISION in the Library of Congress? Is it the three-term senator looking for that nineteenth-century song about his home state, or the elderly woman trying to find the love song her father copyrighted in 1915? Could it be the Dutch professor requesting microfilm copies of several seventeenth-century music theory books, or the New Yorker whose passion is American musical theater? Is it perhaps the graduate student studying the correspondence between a composer and her publisher, or a picture researcher looking for just the right illustrations for a book about chamber music?

Actually, it is all of these, and many more, who visit or write to the world's largest music library every year. Some come looking for one particular book or small scrap of information, while others pursue brief or extended research along broader lines: all of the works and related materials of a certain composer, perhaps, or all of the trios written for flute, viola, and piano. Many visitors are solo artists or ensemble performers seeking—and finding—a treasure trove of new repertoire. Whether the project is large or small, professional, or simply one of personal interest, these patrons turn to the Music Division of the Library of Congress because of the vast, comprehensive, and unique nature of its collections.

Indeed, the breadth and depth of its collections are what set the Music Division apart from other large libraries, both in the United States and abroad. Its holdings stretch from antiphons to zarzuela, from more than 120 songs about the *Titanic* to a magnificent collection of Brahms autograph music manuscripts and letters, from books about harpsichord construction to Paganini's handwritten recipe for ravioli! The Albert Schatz Collection contains more than 12,000 opera librettos, the perfect complement to an outstanding collection of orchestral opera scores. The music and papers of Aaron Copland and Irving Berlin have been wonderful additions to collections already strong in primary resources for both classical and popular American music.

Patrons who come to the Library of Congress to use the collections of the Music Division do so in the Performing Arts Reading Room (PARR) in the Madison Building. Here, readers have at their disposal what sometimes seem to be unlimited resources for their musical research: thousands of scores, music histories, bibliographies, theory books, music journals, microforms, manuscripts (both music and literary), and more ephemeral materials such as scrapbooks, programs, and photographs. Even such a specialized subject as music for silent films is well represented. (Staff member Gillian B. Anderson's *Music for Silent Films, 1894–1929*, has become a well-known source and has revitalized interest in performing the scores during showings of the films.)

Mary Wooton in the Library's Conservation Office treating the autograph manuscript of Arnold Schoenberg's *Pierrot Lunaire*, and a page from the manuscript ("Heimweh") showing a hinged paste-over which has been removed in conservation, and replaced so that its original location and the underlying material can be examined. In this major innovative work of the twentieth century, Schoenberg made his first use of *Sprechstimme*, in which the voice replaces the sung pitches with speech-song. Its premiere evoked as much furor and adverse critical reaction as Stravinsky's *Rite of Spring* (1913). *Pierrot Lunaire* (1912) predates Schoenberg's development of his "method of composing with twelve different notes related entirely to one another," his so-called serial or twelve-tone system. (*Gertrude Clarke Whittall Foundation Collection*) (*Photograph by Jim Higgins*)

Members of the Reader Services staff answer reference questions, search automated networks with other libraries, and assist patrons using the card catalogs, computers, microform readers, and photocopiers. The reference collection in the reading room contains basic music reference books, theater and dance reference sources, and some general reference tools as well.

Nonetheless, because the music collections are so vast—an estimated eight million items—many works, especially smaller forms such as songs, works for one or two instruments, and the like, are not represented by an individual entry in either the card or automated catalogs. These materials can be located, however, with the assistance of the resourceful and skilled reference staff. Patrons may be directed to other areas of the Library—for example, to the public catalogs of the Copyright Office in the Madison Building—to search for further information about works that are not fully cataloged. Indeed, the Library's millions of music copyright deposits document the history of music in the United States as no other materials can—they are yet another treasure trove of unique items.

For decades the Music Division, in conjunction with the Library's Photoduplication Service, has administered an on-site preservation microfilming project to both protect and disseminate materials in its collections. In addition, commercial microforms are added to the collections on an ongoing basis. Readers use these materials in the soundproof multipurpose rooms which line the Performing Arts Reading Room. To enable readers to hear the music they are using, some multipurpose rooms contain one or two pianos for reading through works in the collections. All of the multipurpose rooms are equipped with listening facilities, some with video facilities; researchers consult the Library's Motion Picture, Broadcasting, and Recorded Sound Division to make appointments to listen to recordings or view videorecordings.

The Performing Arts Library (PAL), a section of the Music Division, is located at the nation's John F. Kennedy Center for the Performing Arts. Although

Research in the Performing Arts Reading Room. Scholars studying autograph manuscripts of works by Johannes Brahms. *(Photograph by Reid Baker)*

Joel Sorensen and Linda Fairtile arranging collections in the Acquisitions and Processing Section of the Music Division. Newly acquired materials undergo careful processing to prepare them for use by scholars and the general public. *(Photograph by Reid Baker)*

primarily a reference center, the PAL maintains an extensive research file of materials relating to all of the performing arts, files on all major dance personalities, companies, and genres, and a comprehensive index to the programs *(Stagebill)* of the Kennedy Center that provides rich details about repertory, casting, and program notes for performances at the Kennedy Center since its creation in 1971.

The staff of the PAL, a joint effort of the Library of Congress and the Kennedy Center, comprises specialists in theater and dance who add greatly to the reference service offered in both the PARR and the PAL. Increasingly, the Music Division is enlarging its mission towards providing more resources and more reference service in all areas of the performing arts and in all types of music.

Because the Music Division's collections include so many unique and valuable items, careful conservation and preservation of these treasures are a major consideration. Staff members work closely with the specialists of the Conservation Office so that appropriate treatments and housings are devised for the materials that need them. In addition, the Division also selects items every year for inclusion in preservation microfilming projects. In these efforts, the Music Division seeks to serve its diverse constituents—who share in common a love for some aspect of the musical arts—for many generations to come.

List of Selected Special Collections

The following one hundred Special Collections are drawn from the more than five hundred designated Special Collections in the Music Division. The entries are designed to reveal the most significant materials in each collection.

AMATEUR HOUR COLLECTION. Applications of performers appearing on Major Bowes' Amateur Hour (on radio, 1935–1944) and Ted Mack's Original Amateur Hour (on radio and television, 1948–1968), with accompanying documentation.

AMERICAN HARP SOCIETY REPOSITORY. Manuscript and printed music, photographs, programs, correspondence, periodicals, and scrapbooks documenting the careers of prominent twentieth-century harpists.

GEORGE ANTHEIL COLLECTION. Music manuscripts of the self-styled "Bad Boy of Music," a leading American avant-garde composer of the 1920s and 1930s; Antheil's correspondence with Stanley Hart and Mary Curtis Bok.

ARSIS PRESS ARCHIVES. Music manuscripts, proof copies, and other publishing materials for works published by Arsis Press, devoted to works by women composers; business records dating from its founding in 1974.

ERNST BACON COLLECTION. Autograph music manuscripts and photocopies of Bacon's orchestral, chamber, and larger choral works; literary materials, notebooks, professional and personal correspondence.

SAMUEL BARBER COLLECTION. Autograph music manuscripts and libretto materials; includes extensive holdings for *Antony and Cleopatra,* written for the opening of the new Metropolitan Opera House in New York in 1966.

CHARLIE BARNET COLLECTION. Manuscript jazz orchestrations from the band library of the American saxophonist and leader of a dance band particularly noted for its jazz playing during the 1930s and 1940s.

BÉLA BARTÓK–MARYA FREUND CORRESPONDENCE. Correspondence between Bartók and Marya Freund, a German soprano noted for her performances of modern music.

JOHN DAVIS BATCHELDER COLLECTION. Autograph manuscripts and iconography relating chiefly to nineteenth-century composers and opera singers; includes a lock of Beethoven's hair and a letter written by George Sand about Frédéric Chopin.

Arnold Schoenberg, 1936. *(George and Ira Gershwin Collection) (Photograph by Edward Weston) (Copyright © 1981, Center for Creative Photography, Arizona Board of Regents)*

HAROLD BAUER COLLECTION.
Personal papers, music manuscripts, and photographs of the British-American pianist and writer, for a time president of the Friends of Music in the Library of Congress.

IRVING BERLIN COLLECTION.
Personal papers and scrapbooks of Irving Berlin; the archives of the Irving Berlin Music Corp.; includes manuscripts for such classics as "God Bless America" and "White Christmas."

LEONARD BERNSTEIN COLLECTION.
Music manuscripts, personal papers, and 114 scrapbooks documenting Bernstein's career; includes correspondence with Helen Coates, his first piano teacher, and autograph manuscripts for *West Side Story.*

ERNEST BLOCH COLLECTION. Music manuscripts, correspondence, lecture notes, and business records of the Swiss-born composer, conductor, and teacher who first attracted international attention by winning the Elizabeth Sprague Coolidge prize for his *Suite for Viola and Piano* in 1919.

FRANZISKA BOAS COLLECTION.
Personal and professional papers documenting the career of the American choreographer and teacher, artistic director of the Franziska Boas Dance Company, and a pioneer in the field of dance accompaniment.

WILLIAM BATCHELDER BRADBURY COLLECTION. A musical autograph album (ca. 1850) assembled during his period of study in Europe, containing inscriptions by many prominent musical figures; a letterpress book and other items.

BUDAPEST STRING QUARTET COLLECTION. Manuscript and printed scores and parts, programs, photographs, and other materials relating to the members of the internationally renowned quartet, in residence at the Library of Congress, 1940–1962.

JAMES MADISON CARPENTER COLLECTION. Transcriptions of British and American folk music and folk plays; music manuscripts, song texts, pictorial materials, field notes and related items.

JOHN ALDEN CARPENTER COLLECTION. Manuscript and printed music, correspondence, scrapbooks, clippings, and drawings and photographs of sets and costume designs for works of this twentieth-century jazz-influenced composer.

ELIZABETH SPRAGUE COOLIDGE FOUNDATION COLLECTION. The archives of the Coolidge Foundation including autograph manuscripts of nearly one hundred commissioned works; personal papers, manuscripts of Mrs. Coolidge's compositions and works dedicated to her, photographs, and other items.

AARON COPLAND COLLECTION.
Music manuscripts representing almost every work by Copland; his voluminous correspondence, business records, photographs, subject files, and other materials.

SIDNEY ROBERTSON COWELL COLLECTION. Correspondence, photographs, and field notes of this pioneering ethnomusicologist, the wife of composer Henry Cowell.

DAMROSCH FAMILY COLLECTION.
Personal papers, music materials, correspondence, and scrapbooks documenting the lives of several generations of this American dynasty of musicians.

DIAGHILEV/LIFAR COLLECTION.
Printed and manuscript music from the library of the Russian impresario, later belonging to Sergei Lifar, a principal dancer with the Ballets Russes; correspondence and a notebook kept by Diaghilev during his last years.

VERNON DUKE COLLECTION. Music manuscripts, personal papers, and scrapbooks documenting the work of the Russian emigré who composed art music under his Russian name, Vladimir Dukelsky, and popular music as the American, Vernon Duke.

CARL ENGEL COLLECTION.
Correspondence and business papers of the musicologist and writer; includes papers from his positions as Chief of the Music Division (1922–1934) and president of music publishing company G. Schirmer, Inc.

GERALDINE FARRAR COLLECTION.
Personal papers, scrapbooks, and memorabilia of one of the leading American opera singers of the first decades of the twentieth century, representing her stage, screen, and public service careers.

IRVING FINE COLLECTION. Music materials representing virtually every composition of the American composer and teacher; personal papers, scrapbooks, and ephemera.

BOB FOSSE/GWEN VERDON COLLECTION. Personal papers, photographs, and other materials meticulously documenting the careers of dancer/choreographer Fosse and dancer/singer Verdon.

GEORGE AND IRA GERSHWIN COLLECTION. Music materials, correspondence, photographs, scrapbooks, and other items relating to composer George Gershwin and lyricist Ira Gershwin; includes autograph manuscripts of all of the major Gershwin scores and a self-portrait oil painting of each brother.

ALMA GLUCK COLLECTION.
Scrapbooks documenting the career of this Rumanian-born American soprano; music materials, photographs, correspondence, and ephemera.

LEOPOLD GODOWSKY COLLECTION.
Music manuscripts and personal papers of the Polish-born pianist, including his piano transcriptions of legendary difficulty; business and financial papers, photographs, and printed music.

JULIUS GOLD COLLECTION.
Professional and personal papers of the musicologist, theoretician, and teacher, comprising pedagogical materials and extensive correspondence with his students.

FERDE GROFÉ COLLECTION.
Manuscript and printed music for Grofé's own compositions as well as his arrangements of other composers' works; includes scores for his *Grand Canyon Suite* and his orchestration of Gershwin's *Rhapsody in Blue.*

GLENN DILLARD GUNN COLLECTION.
Correspondence, photographs, clippings, printed music, and other materials deriving from the career of the pianist and music critic, active in Chicago, 1910–1936, and in Washington, 1940–1954.

OSCAR HAMMERSTEIN II COLLEC-TION. Scripts, librettos, correspondence, scrapbooks, music materials, and related items; includes scripts and lyrics for some of the most popular musicals of the twentieth century.

JASCHA HEIFETZ COLLECTION. Manuscript and printed music comprising the performing library of the Russian-born violinist; scrapbooks, photographs, and extensive files of concert repertoire lists and programs.

HEINEMAN FOUNDATION COLLECTION IN HONOR OF EDWARD N. WATERS. Autograph music manuscripts and correspondence and rare imprints; includes a copy of the first printed libretto of Handel's *Messiah* and a copy of Tinctoris's *Terminorum Musicae Diffinitorium*, the first printed dictionary of musical terms (ca. 1495).

VICTOR HERBERT COLLECTION. Music scores and orchestral parts, librettos, scrapbooks, programs, and photographs of the Irish-born, German-educated American cellist, conductor, and composer.

IRENE HESKES COLLECTION. Sheet music of Yiddish popular songs spanning the years 1895–1950, much of it from the archives of the Hebrew Publishing Company.

GEORGE HODGES COLLECTION. The music libraries of Hodges's father and grandfather, comprising eighteenth- and nineteenth-century manuscript and printed music, instructional materials, pamphlets, and other materials, mostly of English origin.

CARRIE JACOBS-BOND COLLECTION. Music manuscripts, personal papers, photographs, and business records of the printing house which she established for her own works.

CHARLES JAHANT COLLECTION. Nearly two thousand photographs of opera singers, dating from the late nineteenth century to the present; many are inscribed to Mr. Jahant.

DANNY KAYE AND SYLVIA FINE KAYE COLLECTION. A comprehensive archive of the compositions of Sylvia Fine Kaye, many of them written for Danny Kaye's film and stage appearances; scripts, music, and business records relating to his television shows.

JEROME KERN COLLECTION. Music materials dating from the beginning of his career through the 1930s; orchestrations for many important works including comprehensive holdings for *Show Boat.*

HANS KINDLER FOUNDATION COLLECTION. Music materials and business records of the Kindler Foundation which chronicle its concert and commissioning activities; Kindler's personal papers and manuscript and printed scores.

OTTO KLEMPERER COLLECTION. Music materials, correspondence, photographs, and books from his personal library; research materials relating to Peter Heyworth's biography of Klemperer.

ERICH WOLFGANG KORNGOLD COLLECTION. Autograph manuscript scores for most of the works of the Austrian-born composer of concert music and film scores; correspondence and ephemera.

ANDRE KOSTELANETZ COLLECTION. Manuscript orchestrations used by the Russian-born conductor; personal papers, correspondence, and books from his personal library; American music materials purchased through his bequest.

KOUSSEVITZKY ARCHIVES. Music materials and personal papers of the Russian conductor; the archives of the Koussevitzky Foundation, documenting a fifty-year commissioning program; includes manuscripts of more than 250 commissioned works.

FRITZ KREISLER COLLECTION. Manuscript scores for works by Kreisler as well as his arrangements of works by other composers; correspondence, photographs, biographical materials; his Guarneri del Gesù violin and the autograph manuscript of Brahms's *Violin Concerto in D major.*

HARRY AND SARAH LEPMAN COLLECTION. American patriotic sheet music from the 1890s though World War II, many items having highly decorative covers.

CHARLES MARTIN TORNOV LOEFFLER COLLECTION. Correspondence, music manuscripts, photographs, programs, and clippings spanning the entire career of this Alsatian-born composer and violinist.

PAUL LÖWENBERG COLLECTION. More than 1,600 first edition piano scores of Viennese dance music, including nearly all the works by composers of the Lanner and Strauss families, the nineteenth-century "waltz kings" of Vienna.

EDWARD AND MARIAN MACDOWELL COLLECTION. Music materials and personal papers of Edward MacDowell; materials pertaining to his wife, Marian MacDowell, and to the MacDowell Colony, which she established in New Hampshire.

JOHN HERBERT MCDOWELL COLLECTION. Manuscript and printed music, photographs, programs, and personal papers documenting the career of the American composer who wrote chiefly for the theater and dance.

MCKIM FUND COLLECTION. Personal papers of Leonora Jackson McKim, one of the first women to achieve international recognition as a concert violinist; the archives of the McKim Fund, established to support music for violin and piano; includes manuscripts of nearly forty commissioned works.

LORETTA C. MANGGRUM COLLECTION. Music scores, programs, and other materials of the African-American composer, teacher, and church musician.

MASON/MCCONATHY COLLECTION. Nineteenth-century European school music books, collected by Lowell Mason and later organized by his student, Osborne McConathy.

NIKOLAI KARLOVICH MEDTNER COLLECTION. Manuscript and printed music, professional and family correspondence, books, and a plaster cast of the hands of the Russian pianist and composer.

DAYTON C. MILLER COLLECTION. More than 1,600 flutes and related instruments, music, iconography, memorabilia, and Dr. Miller's 3,000-volume library containing virtually every publication on the flute and flute playing issued up to 1940.

CHARLES MINGUS COLLECTION. Autograph manuscripts of composer, bassist, and bandleader Mingus; photographs, literary manuscripts, correspondence, and tape recordings of interviews, broadcasts, recording sessions, and Mingus composing at the piano.

MODERN MUSIC ARCHIVES. Business records of *Modern Music,* a journal that championed the cause of contemporary music (1924–1946); correspondence, typescripts of articles, and photographs.

MOLDENHAUER ARCHIVES AT THE LIBRARY OF CONGRESS. Autograph music manuscripts, correspondence, literary documents, and other primary source materials spanning the entire history of Western music, from Gregorian chant to the twentieth century.

FERDINAND "JELLY ROLL" MORTON COLLECTION. Manuscript and printed copyright deposit scores, chiefly from the 1920s and 1930s.

NATIONAL NEGRO OPERA COMPANY COLLECTION. Photographs, clippings, correspondence, and other materials documenting performers and performances of the Washington-based company, active from the late 1930s until the early 1960s.

NEWLAND/ZEUNER COLLECTION. The music libraries of Philadelphia musicians William Newland and Charles Zeuner, comprising manuscript and printed music of the late eighteenth and nineteenth centuries: sacred choral music, songs, and chamber and orchestral music.

RACHMANINOFF ARCHIVES. Autograph music manuscripts, personal papers, correspondence, and memorabilia documenting the career of the composer, pianist, and conductor, chiefly after his emigration from Russia in 1917.

MRS. GILES F. RICH COLLECTION. Scrapbooks containing programs, photographs, ticket stubs, and other memorabilia documenting musical, theatrical, and athletic events in and around Boston, 1882–1953.

RICHARD RODGERS COLLECTION. Autograph music manuscripts for many of Rodgers's best known works written with lyricists Lorenz Hart and Oscar Hammerstein II; includes *Babes in Arms, South Pacific,* and *Oklahoma!*

SIGMUND ROMBERG COLLECTION. Manuscript and printed music, librettos, film scripts, and photographs of Romberg, one of the most prolific writers of popular music of the twentieth century; includes *The New Moon* and *The Student Prince.*

ROSENTHAL COLLECTION. Autograph music and literary manuscripts collected by Harry Rosenthal; includes rich holdings of autograph music manuscripts and correspondence of Franz Liszt.

ARTUR RUBINSTEIN COLLECTION. Correspondence, photographs, concert and repertoire documents, business records, and related materials, largely after 1940.

FRANCIS MARIA SCALA COLLECTION. Manuscript and printed band music, chiefly composed or arranged by Scala, the first Leader of the Marine Band, 1855–1871; includes an autograph note to Scala from Abraham Lincoln.

ALBERT SCHATZ COLLECTION. More than twelve thousand printed opera librettos dating from 1601 through the nineteenth century; research materials compiled by Schatz.

ARTHUR P. SCHMIDT COMPANY ARCHIVES. The archives of the Boston music publisher, which handled virtually all significant American composers from the late nineteenth through the mid-twentieth centuries; autograph music manuscripts, printed music, and business records.

ARTUR SCHNABEL COLLECTION. Autograph music manuscripts of the Austrian-born pianist, composer, and teacher; materials for his edition of Beethoven sonatas.

ARNOLD SCHOENBERG COLLECTION. Correspondence to Schoenberg as well as carbon copies of letters from Schoenberg; extensive exchanges with his two most famous pupils, Alban Berg and Anton von Webern.

WILLIAM HOWARD SCHUMAN COLLECTION. Autograph manuscripts for chamber, symphonic, and operatic works; libretto material; includes *The Mighty Casey.*

IRVING SCHWERKÉ COLLECTION. Correspondence, autograph albums, photograph albums, and scrapbooks, spanning the entire career of this American writer on music.

CHARLES AND RUTH CRAWFORD SEEGER COLLECTION. Music manuscripts, printed materials, correspondence, and other papers deriving from the work of musicologist/ethnomusicologist Charles Seeger and his wife, composer Ruth Crawford Seeger.

GISELA SELDEN-GOTH COLLECTION. Autograph music manuscripts of eminent eighteenth-, nineteenth-, and twentieth-century European composers, collected by the Hungarian musicologist and composer.

ROGER SESSIONS COLLECTION. Autograph music manuscripts and personal and professional papers; includes literary materials for his opera, *Montezuma.*

ELIE SIEGMEISTER COLLECTION. Manuscript and printed music materials, libretti, educational materials, clippings, and correspondence.

BEVERLY SILLS COLLECTION. Forty-one scrapbooks documenting the career and contributions of one of twentieth-century America's most important singers and a leader in music administration.

NICOLAS SLONIMSKY COLLECTION. Papers of the musical lexicographer, conductor, and composer best known for his exhaustive work on editions of Baker's *Biographical Dictionary of Musicians;* manuscripts of more than twenty compositions by Slonimsky; printed materials from his library.

OSCAR GEORGE THEODORE SONNECK COLLECTION. Papers of the first Chief of the Music Division, 1902–1917, including research notes, publication materials, and correspondence; the major portion of the collection comprises his correspondence as founding editor of the *Musical Quarterly.*

JOHN PHILIP SOUSA COLLECTION. Autograph music manuscripts for most of the works of the American composer and conductor; includes "The Stars and Stripes Forever," officially designated as the national march of the United States.

HANS SPIALEK COLLECTION.
Manuscript and printed scores and parts for works composed or orchestrated by Spialek; diaries, correspondence, ephemera, and photographs; music materials belonging to Spialek and to his wife, singer Dora Boshoer.

HAROLD AND ROSE MARIE SPIVACKE COLLECTION. Personal, professional, and student papers of Harold Spivacke, Chief of the Music Division, 1937–1972; rarities purchased with funds bequeathed by Mrs. Spivacke, including autograph correspondence of Alban Berg.

EDWARD AND CLARA STEUERMANN COLLECTION. Manuscript and printed music, correspondence, and other materials relating to pianist and composer Edward Steuermann; papers of his wife, music librarian Clara Steuermann.

STRAVINSKY/CRAFT COLLECTION. Publishers' proofs and photocopies of works by Stravinsky, many with extensive autograph corrections and annotations, given to the Library by Stravinsky's protégé, conductor and writer Robert Craft.

WILLIAM REMSEN STRICKLAND COLLECTION. Printed music, photographs, scrapbooks, correspondence, promotional materials, and ephemera of the conductor noted for his performances of American music.

HENRYK SZERYNG COLLECTION. Personal papers, manuscript and printed music, photographs, scrapbooks; includes Szeryng's reconstruction of Paganini's *Third Violin Concerto.*

TAMS-WITMARK RENTAL SCORE COLLECTION. The music firm's rental score collection of nearly seven thousand manuscript and printed scores for operas and operettas dating from the early nineteenth to the early twentieth centuries.

VLADIMIR USSACHEVSKY COLLECTION. Personal papers, educational materials, and music manuscripts of this innovator in the field of electronic music and one of the founders of the Columbia-Princeton Electronic Music Center.

HARRY VON TILZER COLLECTION. Music manuscripts, lyric sheets, scripts, and business records of the Harry Von Tilzer Music Co., one of the most successful American popular-music publishers of the early twentieth century; includes extensive autograph materials of Von Tilzer.

SAMUEL PROWSE WARREN COLLECTION. Programs from performances given chiefly in churches in the New York City area, ca. 1880–1910; important turn-of-the-century programs from major New York concert halls.

EDWARD N. AND LILLY L. WATERS COLLECTION. Autograph letters and first editions of the music of Franz Liszt from the estate of Edward Waters, Chief of the Music Division, 1972–1976; his research notes relating to Victor Herbert; correspondence.

HUGO WEISGALL COLLECTION. Music and literary manuscripts of the composer and theorist; includes personal correspondence during World War II.

GERTRUDE CLARKE WHITTALL COLLECTION. The quintet of Stradivari instruments given by Mrs. Whittall; autograph manuscripts of prominent European composers; includes notable manuscripts of Brahms, and documentary holdings of Paganini and Mendelssohn; the archives of the Whittall Foundation.